ETHNIC
AMERICA

edited by MARJORIE P. K. WEISER

THE REFERENCE SHELF
Volume 50   Number 2

THE H. W. WILSON COMPANY
New York   1978

THE REFERENCE SHELF

The books in this series contain reprints of articles, excerpts from books, and addresses on current issues and social trends in the United States and other countries. There are six separately bound numbers in each volume, all of which are generally published in the same calendar year. One number is a collection of recent speeches; each of the others is devoted to a single subject and gives background information and discussion from various points of view, concluding with a comprehensive bibliography. Books in the series may be purchased individually or on subscription.

Copyright © 1978
By The H. W. Wilson Company
PRINTED IN THE UNITED STATES OF AMERICA

Library of Congress Cataloging in Publication Data
Main entry under title:

Ethnic America.

(The Reference shelf ; v. 50, no. 2)

Bibliography: p .
SUMMARY: A compilation of reprinted articles considering various ethnic groups in the United States, with emphasis on Native Americans and Afro-Americans, and how they coped with their problems in adjusting to the dominant culture.
1. Minorities—United States—Addresses, essays, lectures. 2. Ethnicity—Addresses, essays, lectures. [1. Minorities—Addresses, essays, lectures. 2. Ethnicity—Addresses, essays, lectures] I. Weiser, Marjorie P. K. II. Series.

E184.A1E777   301.45′1′0973   78-16269
ISBN 0-8242-0623-1

PREFACE

From Estonia to Ecuador, from Kenya to Korea, no corner of the globe is unrepresented in the population mix that is the United States of America. There are European-Americans, Afro-Americans, Asian-Americans, Pacific Americans, Latin-American Americans, and Native Americans, all of them further subdivided into many national groups, each with its distinct traditions. Language, religious practices, and other culture traits are part of the baggage with which people arrive in a new land. As the world's governments and economies shift in every generation—every decade—new groups of people, in our time mostly refugees from repressive regimes, depart the lands of their birth to start life over again. Cubans, Haitians, Vietnamese, Thais, and Soviet Jews are among the most recent emigrés.

A group of people of the same race or national origin, speaking the same language and/or sharing a common and distinctive culture, is an ethnic group. Common racial identity alone does not characterize an ethnic group; a sharing of history and cultural tradition is required.

Ethnicity "counts." It is significant on several levels. First, membership in a particular group is an integral part of self-identity, an important component of everyone's answer to the question "Who are you?" Ethnicity may determine what you eat for breakfast, what you wear to a funeral, when you celebrate a holy day, what career you plan for, whom you marry, where you live, and whom you choose as friends. Ethnicity counts in other ways as well. It has become a focus for political organization in the United States and in countries throughout the world. In Biafra and Bangladesh, in Nazi Germany and in South Africa, in Lebanon and in Northern Ireland, and in dozens of other lands, ethnicity has literally been a matter of life and death. Less extremely, in our own country, ethnicity can be a matter of lobbying and pressure groups, union membership, housing availability, career opportunity, school curriculum changes, and elections won or lost. An ethnic group has been described by the sociologist Arnold W. Green as "a foreign-stock segment of the population which preserves in some degree a distinctive way of life, in language, mannerism, habit, loyalty and the like."

In preserving its distinctiveness, an ethnic group becomes a noticeable minority group. A minority has subordinate status within the larger society and most of its distinguishing characteristics are considered undesirable by the dominant group; minority-group identity or self-awareness is intensified both by these shared characteristics and by the discrimination that results from them. Members of minority groups tend to marry members of the same group, and minority-group membership is acquired at birth, automatically, and transmitted to future generations.

Jacob Riis, the late nineteenth century Danish-born crusader against appalling slum conditions, declared "There is no flag like the flag of my fathers, save only that of my children and of my manhood." He called his autobiography *The Making of an American,* and this title and statement reflect his determination to enjoy full participation in his adopted land. He achieved it, too—and, while trying to prod and inspire other ethnic immigrants to follow his road to full Americanization, disparaged them in the process. Riis was a talented journalist and ardent reformer, but his own progress was undoubtedly aided by his northern European origin, Protestant religious affiliation, and fair complexion, characteristics he shared with the majority of Americans. The more noticeable and more exotic darker Europeans and nonwhite ethnics did not blend so easily physically and had more distinctively different traditions culturally.

Minority-group members have often been accorded less than equal treatment, but especially in recent years ethnic groups have tended to respond to discrimination by a militant self-awareness—in a way, they are coming out of a collective identity crisis. Since the end of the Second World War, a new ethnic awareness has manifested itself. Never before have so many Americans asserted their distinctive group affiliations or formed study groups and more formal organizations to explore the meanings of their diverse origins and to put forward their claims on the public consciousness. Writers and speakers from every conceivable background appear in magazines and newspapers and on television to call national attention to one issue or another. On a congressional level, there have been laws to fund ethnic heritage studies and projects and to provide multilingual elections materials. On a daily-life level, people are exploring such things as ethnic arts and crafts and international cookery. We may be enriched, though at times confused, by the ethnic variety that surrounds us.

This book surveys the ethnic diversity of the United States, touching on some of its implications for all Americans. In the first section, three selections combine to present an overview of this complex topic: first, a survey of immigration; next, a historical explanation of the ways in which the uniquely American experience has been the heritage of its multiple components; and lastly, a poignant statement of the "double bind" experienced by all Americans who would preserve the uniqueness of their ethnic heritage while participating fully in the United States they live in.

The second section presents a variety of ethnic experiences—a small sampling from the vast store of material available. In the third section are articles dealing with Native Americans—the ethnic group (or groups) confronted by and in conflict with the European settlers whose culture was to be the dominant one of the new nation. These natives, misnamed "Indians" by the Europeans, were themselves descendants of immigrants, but immigrants whose arrival in the Western Hemisphere antedated recorded history. The fourth section is devoted to the special social and cultural problems faced by the only immigrant group to arrive unwillingly, in chains—Afro-Americans.

In the final section the contemporary resurgence of ethnic consciousness, dubbed the "new ethnicity," is presented, along with some appraisals of this rediscovery for the political and social future of the nation.

Space limitations make it impossible to represent every ethnic group and every point of view, but selections have been chosen to give a variety of perspectives on a complex and many-faceted topic. For other experiences or points of view, the reader is directed to additional sources listed in the bibliography at the end of this volume.

The compiler thanks those writers and publishers who have granted permission to reprint the selections in this volume.

MARJORIE P. K. WEISER

May 1978

CONTENTS

I. NATION OF IMMIGRANTS, NATION OF ETHNICS: AN OVERVIEW

EDITOR'S INTRODUCTION

Whatever their ethnic background, all Americans have in common the fact that their ancestors (or they themselves) came to North America from somewhere else; as a result we live in the midst of an ethnic diversity unmatched in any other nation. The United States Bureau of the Census provides statistical verification (see pages 12–13).

Approximately 7 out of every 8 persons in the United States are descendants of European immigrants, 1 out of every 9 is descended from African immigrants, and 1 in 100 is a descendant of American Indians or of immigrants from Asian countries. As the statistics indicate, in 1970, with the population at 203.2 million, 9.6 million or 4.7 percent were foreign born (first generation) and 23.9 million or 11.8 percent were born to a foreign-born parent or foreign-born parents (second generation). That made for a total of 33.6 million persons who were first- or second-generation Americans (or "foreign stock," as the Census Bureau calls them). Native-born persons whose parents were also native-born constituted the remaining 169.6 million, or 83.5 percent of the population. Of these "native-native" persons, one eighth were black and nearly seven eighths were white, with less than 1 percent of Asian, American Indian, or other racial origin. Among these other racial groups the 1970 census identified four smaller ones: 100,000 Hawaiians, 66,000 Koreans, and 28,000 Eskimos and 6,000 Aleuts in Alaska.

Race, however, is not ethnicity, although there are correlations. American blacks are, by definition, Afro-American; but those blacks who might prefer to ignore their African heritage are nonetheless, by reason of their obvious racial identity, assigned to the same ethnic group as those who readily embrace that heritage. On the other hand,

FOREIGN STOCK BY COUNTRY OF ORIGIN: 1970
(in millions)

Country of Origin	Total Foreign Stock	Foreign Born	Native, of Foreign or Mixed Parentage
All Countries	33.575	9.619	23.956
Europe and USSR	23.551	5.712	17.841
United Kingdom (England, Scotland, Wales, Northern Ireland)	2.465	.686	1.779
Ireland	1.45	.251	1.199
Other Northwestern Europe (Norway, Sweden, Denmark, Netherlands, Belgium, Switzerland, France)	2.823	.593	2.230
Germany	3.622	.833	2.789
Poland	2.374	.548	1.826
Other Central Europe (Czechoslovakia, Austria, Hungary, Yugoslavia)	2.786	.712	2.074
Eastern Europe (Latvia, Estonia, Lithuania, Finland, Rumania, Bulgaria)	.878	.254	.624
Italy	4.241	1.008	3.233
Other Southern Europe (Greece, Spain, Portugal)	.829	.327	.502
USSR	1.943	.463	1.480
All other Europe	.140	.037	.103
Asia	1.745	.824	.921
Turkey	.107	.048	.059

China	.339	.172	.167
Japan	.394	.120	.274
Philippine Islands	.350	.185	.165
Other Asia (Lebanon, Israel, Syria, Pakistan, India, Korea, all other Asia)	.555	.299	.256
North and Central America	6.506	2.360	4.146
Canada	3.034	.812	2.222
Mexico	2.339	.760	1.579
Central America (Guatemala, British Honduras, Honduras, Nicaragua, El Salvador, Costa Rica, Panama)	.188	.113	.075
Caribbean and West Indies (Cuba, Jamaica, British West Indies, Dominican Republic, Haiti, Trinidad and Tobago, and other West Indies)	.945	.675	.270
South America (Colombia, Venezuela, Ecuador, Peru, Brazil, Bolivia, Uruguay, Chile, Argentina, other South America)	.389	.255	.134
Africa, Atlantic and Pacific Islands	.340	.151	.189
Country Not Specified	1.044	.317	.727

American Indians share a racial identity but derive from numerous distinct ethnic traditions. (See Introductions to Sections III and IV.)

In 1900 there were more foreign-born persons in the United States, and they constituted a much larger proportion of the total population, than in 1970. The proportion of foreign-born was 15 percent in 1900, the highest on record. The actual number of foreign-born reached its record high of 14.3 million in 1930; this constituted only 12 percent of the total population in that year, however. Whatever their nation of origin, the vast majority of immigrants have hastened to become part of their adopted nation. Of 1970's 9,739,723 foreign-born, 6,198,173 had become naturalized.

As R. C. Schroeder points out in the first article in this section, all Americans, including the Native Americans or Indians, are immigrants. Immigration as a source of population has its strengths and weaknesses. Among the latter must be counted the prolonged period of adjustment to the new world, a period in which the differences between newcomers and old settlers are often disturbingly noticeable. During periods of heaviest immigration, economic factors coincided with the universal tendency to exalt one's own group and downgrade noticeable "others," frequently resulting in an antiforeign movement.

But since virtually all immigrants continued to become an integral part of the nation, a distinctive American ethos or character was created. George W. Pierson, in the second selection, brings up to date the perception of "the American, this new man" first articulated nearly two hundred years ago by the writer Crèvecœur. Pierson notes a number of factors that acted upon all of America's ethnics to shape what he calls the "new version of Western civilization" that exists in the United States.

The last selection is from W. E. B. Du Bois' famous book *The Souls of Black Folk*. This excerpt deals with the discovery that one is different and of the extra burden imposed throughout life as a consequence. Du Bois was writing of his experience as a member of the black minority in a predominantly white America. Yet when he says, "One ever feels his twoness," he expresses a feeling shared by all people—Italians and Filipinos, Puerto Ricans and Poles, Chinese and Chicanos, and countless other groups —who have ever been made to feel different or unwanted, who are always aware of the double cultural heritage they bear.

THE IMMIGRANT HERITAGE OF AMERICA [1]

We are, in the words of John F. Kennedy, "a nation of immigrants." With one exception, all Americans are descended from foreigners who arrived on these shores within the past four centuries. The exception is the full-blooded American Indian. His forebears also immigrated, from Asia, but thousands of years earlier. Since 1607, when the first permanent English settlers reached the New World, at Jamestown, fully 44 million people have immigrated to what is now the United States—one of the largest movements of people in recorded history. In his classic study of immigration, *The Uprooted* (1951), Oscar Handlin wrote: "Once I thought to write a history of the immigrants in America. Then I discovered that the immigrants *were* American history."

Most immigrants came of peasant stock. In some cases, they were fleeing intolerable conditions at home—religious persecution in the case of the Jews; famine, in the case of the Irish after 1845. But most were lured by the promise of a new and rapidly growing nation, by the limitless horizons of the American frontier, and by the insatiable hunger of a burgeoning industrial machine for more hands, muscles and minds.

In the 130 years between 1820 and 1950, the largest single group in American immigration was the Germans. Some 6.2 million were admitted to the United States. They are followed by Italians (nearly 5 million); Irish (4.6 million); and British (4 million). The Austrian and Russian Empires together contributed 8 million—Poles, Jews, Hungarians,

[1] From "Ethnic America," by Richard C. Schroeder, staff writer. *Editorial Research Reports.* v 1, no 3:52-9. Ja. 20, '71. Reprinted by permission.

Bohemians, Slovaks, Ukrainians and Ruthenians. From the Balkans and Asia Minor came 3 million more—Greeks, Macedonians, Croatians, Albanians, Syrians and Armenians —and from Scandinavia 2 million.

Marcus Lee Hansen, a noted historian of immigration, divides the inflow into three major periods: 1820-1860, which he characterizes as "Celtic" (Scots, Irish, Welsh, and Germans from the Upper Rhine Valley); 1860-1890 "Teutonic" (Prussians, Saxons, Bohemians, Scandinavians); and 1890-1914, a mixture of "Mediterranean" and "Slavic." The decade of peak flow was 1901-1910, when almost 8.8 million immigrants reached these shores. In the following decade, World War I reduced immigration to a trickle for nearly five years, but the ten-year total still reached 5.7 million.

Varied Homelands of Earliest Settlers in America

"Three ships which discovered America sailed under a Spanish flag, were commanded by an Italian sea captain, and included in their crews an Englishman, an Irishman, a Jew and a Negro." Kennedy, the future President, thus described how, from the beginning, America has been a potpourri of races and nations. The Thirteen Colonies were a British-controlled enclave, surrounded by Spanish to the south and southwest and French in the north and west. Within the colonies, the ethnic mix was rich and varied.

The Dutch settled New Amsterdam and explored the Hudson River. Swedes came to Delaware. Polish, German and Italian craftsmen were eagerly solicited to join the struggling Virginia colonists. Germans and Swiss opened up the back country in Pennsylvania, New York, Virginia and the Carolinas. French Huguenots took root in New England, New York, South Carolina and Georgia. The Scots and Irish were in the vanguard that advanced the frontier beyond the Alleghenies. When Britain conquered New Amsterdam in 1664, Kennedy wrote, it offered citizenship to immigrants of eighteen nationalities.

There were also more than two thousand Jews in the colonies, most of them of Sephardic stock, from Spain and Portugal, although the first recorded Jewish settler in Manhattan was a man named Jacob Barsimson who arrived in 1654, and was an Ashkenazic, or German Jew. Descendants of the prerevolutionary Sephardim include such noted American names as Cardozo, Baruch, Lazarus and Nathan. Among these early Americans, there were also Welshmen, who have left behind place names like Bryn Mawr; Waldensian Protestants from northern Italy; Swedes, who taught the colonists how to build log cabins; and untold numbers of black slaves from Africa. (The first cargo of Negroes was landed in Virginia in 1619, but it was not until some 40 years later that perpetual slavery became legally distinct from the temporary servitude of many white immigrants. The importation of slaves was made illegal after 1807.) In the broadest sense, Negroes are the most important of all American ethnic groups. . . . [As of January 1, 1970, according to a Census Bureau estimate] they account for about 23 million Americans, roughly 11 percent of the country's population.

By the time the first federal census was taken in 1790, the population of the United States was already remarkably diverse in its origins. The surnames of heads of families indicate that about 60 percent were of English descent, 14 percent Scottish or Scotch-Irish, 9 percent German, 4 percent Catholic Irish, and 13 percent of various other origins. Wars in Europe and America between 1775 and 1815 brought a forty-year hiatus to New World immigration. But upon resuming, it continued in great waves for more than a century until dammed up, first by World War I and then by restrictive US legislation in the 1920s.

Tidal Waves of Immigration in the Nineteenth Century

Beginning around 1820, the Irish led the first of the great migratory waves that flooded America for the next century. Irish immigration built to a peak after the great famines of 1846-48, reaching a total of nearly one million persons in the following decade. Mostly country folk in their own land, they became city dwellers here. They worked as unskilled laborers, supplying the muscle that built railroads, dug mines and ran mills.

Rejected from the first by "native" Americans, largely because of their Catholic religion, the Irish took refuge in big-city politics, and in a rich and fanciful world of folklore and folk heroes. The archetypal Irish-American hero was John L. Sullivan, heavyweight champion of the world from 1882 to 1892. In his defiant boast of being able to lick any man alive, the Irish found voice and pride in self that had been withheld from them by American society.

Starting about 1830, immigration from Germany paralleled and overlapped that of the Irish. The Germans were a diffuse group, including Lutherans, Catholics and Jews. Although poor, they had more resources than the destitute Irish peasants, and consequently were able to disperse more widely, spreading throughout the Midwest. Sizable German populations and influence still may be found even in such cities as Cincinnati, Cleveland, Milwaukee, Minneapolis and St. Louis.

Politically conservative, the Germans were also anti-slavery. Between 1845 and the outbreak of the Civil War in 1861, 1.25 million Germans arrived, and they were in the forefront of the movement that created the national Republican party. The decade of peak German immigration, the 1880s when 1.5 million arrived, assured "Republican domination of national politics from 1896 to 1930 as much as any other single factor."

The last great nineteenth century immigrant group was the Scandinavians, principally Swedes. This group began arriving in America about 1840, and settled mainly in the upper Mississippi Valley where soil and climatic conditions approximated those of their homelands. In the peak year of 1882 some 100,000 Scandinavian settlers arrived. Primarily rural people, farmers and artisans, Scandinavians settled on the land. Their descendants form an important political group in Minnesota, Iowa, Michigan, Illinois, Nebraska, the Dakotas and Wisconsin.

Last of Massive Arrivals; Hardships En Route

Parents and grandparents of today's troubled ethnic Americans arrived in this country mainly in the last great migratory wave, 1890 to 1914. They came almost entirely from eastern and southern Europe, most of them peasants displaced from their land, suffering from the rapid transition of the rural economies of the Austro-Hungarian and Russian empires, or from the impoverishment of overcrowded Italy.

These were rural folk but, without resources, they were condemned to be packed into the tenements of the great cities of the Northeast and Midwest. Most of them settled within a triangle formed by St. Louis, Boston and Washington. Socially, the United States was ill prepared to receive them; life for the immigrant at the turn of the century was harsher even than it had been for the Irish fifty years earlier. But the mills, factories and sweatshops happily opened their doors to these low-wage, unskilled, but willing workers. Among the eastern Europeans were Czechs, Slovaks, Austrians, Finns, Russians, Poles, Lithuanians, Hungarians, Rumanians, Serbs and Croats. There were also large numbers of Jews from several countries.

From southern Europe came Italians, the largest of the groups, and Greeks. For all the immigrants, the motivation was substantially the same: life in the old country was harsh and the future was bleak. Peasant land-holdings shrank with each succeeding generation and the soil was depleted. America held the promise of better things, if not for the immigrants, then for their descendants.

They came, therefore, in ever-increasing numbers. Between 1905 and 1914, America received an annual average of more than one million immigrants, two thirds of whom came from eastern and southern Europe. The immigrant stream also included Orientals, mainly Japanese and Chinese. Nearly three quarters of a million crossed the Pacific to the US West Coast. They are, properly speaking, a distinct ethnic group, but they do not form part of the movement of blue-collar ethnic workers in the northern and northeastern states.

The immigrant suffered untold deprivation to make his way to this country. He sold his possessions, gave up his village, his homeland, and often his family. He made the long

ocean voyage in cramped steerage, fighting cholera, small
pox and dysentery, frequently without sufficient food an
water. One immigrant in ten died during passage. And ye
they came, in the words of Emma Lazarus (1849-87) inscribe
on the Statue of Liberty, "huddled masses yearning t
breathe free."

Hostility to Newcomers; Immigration Restrictions

But instead of utopia, they often found hostility awai
ing them. Nativism and xenophobia have been persister
aspects of American character throughout history. In i
various manifestations, nativism has been anti-Catholi
anti-radical, anti-Bolshevik, and, most recently, racial. A
though hatred and suspicion of the foreigner have frequentl
been strongest among second-generation Americans, n
tivism at heart presumes that "the United States belongs i
some special sense to the Anglo-Saxon 'race' " and that th
key to national greatness lies in such an identification. N
tivism reached a peak with the meteoric rise and fall of th
anti-immigrant Know-Nothing Party in the 1850s.

Nonetheless, US immigration policy throughout th
nineteenth century was an open door, with virtually no r
strictions on the flow of newcomers. (The most glaring e
ception to the open-door policy was the Oriental Exclusic
Act, severely restricting Chinese immigration, enacted
1882 and renewed in 1892. Chinese immigration was inde
nitely suspended in 1902. Other lesser exceptions were la
barring lunatics, idiots, convicts, and those likely to becom
public charges (1882); the Foran Act, which prohibited tl
importation of contract labor (1885); and general heal
qualifications (1891).) Nativism bubbled up again duri
the great immigrations of 1890-1914. In 1917, Congr
passed—over President Wilson's veto—the first act that se
ously limited immigration. It established literacy tests i
immigrants. As anti-immigrant sentiment continued to r
during the "Red Scare" after World War I, Congress
1921 approved an "emergency" quota system to limit a

nual immigration from all countries outside the Western Hemisphere to 357,000. The open door was closing.

New temporary quotas were set up in 1924, cutting the flow to 164,000 a year. A permanent quota system, placing the limit at 156,981, was adopted in 1929. Each country's quota was based on the number of persons of that national origin who had been in the United States in 1920. This favored the British, Germans and Irish at the expense of southern and eastern Europeans, Asians and Africans. In the next thirty-five years, waiting lists grew longer in Italy, Greece, and Spain, among other countries.

A new immigration law in 1965 finally removed the national quotas and allocated an over-all quota of 170,000 to immigrants from outside the Western Hemisphere. Persons possessing special labor skills, with relatives in the United States or in need of political asylum would be given preference. Nationality would be no factor. For Canada and Latin America, a limit (120,000) was imposed for the first time. Their immigrants would be accepted on a first-come, first-served basis, again without regard to nationality.

Since the law has become effective (Jan. 1, 1966, for immigration from Europe, Africa and Asia; July 1, 1968, for the Western Hemisphere) immigration has undergone a striking change. The British, Germans and Irish have found entry more difficult while arrivals from Greece, Italy, India and the Philippines have multiplied. According to the US Immigration and Naturalization Service, between fiscal years 1965 and 1970, Greek immigration grew from 6,000 to 16,500; Italian from 10,800 to 24,000; Indian from 582 to 10,000; and Philippine from 3,100 to 31,000.

The enlarged immigration from eastern and southern Europe seems destined to reinforce ethnic communities built up around the turn of the century. Nothing approaching that flow can be reached again, however, and changes in the present law aimed at eliminating remaining inequities are not likely to have much effect on the over-all trend established in the past few years.

THE SHAPING OF A PEOPLE:
THE UNITED STATES OF AMERICA [2]

"Americans?" We Americans began as exported Englishmen, or Europeans once removed. With time added to distance, or after five generations of living on these remote shores, we became Anglo-Americans: call us Europeans twice removed. Heated by the fires of rebellion, and we could declare that we were no longer Englishmen at all but Americans: which meant a third removal or kind of separation. Yet meanwhile we had been absorbing handfuls or even considerable numbers of other Europeans called Dutchmen, Swedes, French, Germans, Welsh and Scotch Irish. And then in the nineteenth century would come the second and third great waves of immigration—led by the Catholic Irish and the Germans and the Scandinavians after 1830, then by the peoples from central and southeastern Europe from the 1880s. So by the twentieth century we would be more European than ever, in blood and in mixture of social inheritance. Indeed the peoples of Asia and Africa today seem to see us as *westernism* personified: the pure essence of those European skills and powers and ideas which they most envy or fear.

Yet, for all their intuitions the fact remains that from the first settlements, and increasingly thereafter, we have differed from Europe. In the New World there came to be a New Version of Europe. . . . Perhaps the United States Bicentennial offers a good occasion to reconsider this new, this *American* version, and to ask ourselves once again how and why it got established.

This is an old and honorable inquiry. So we may well begin by recalling some celebrated American explanations.

There was first the great Puritan or Protestant-Dissenter revelation: that we were the Elect—the Chosen People—nation sifted out of the corruption of Europe and favored and watched over by the Lord. . . .

There came next the National-Democratic Vision: that

[2] From an article "Cultural Trends III: American Themes," by George W. Pierson, historian. *Cultures.* v 3, no 3:13–27. '76. © Unesco 1976. Reprinted by permission of Unesco.

America was the land of the free—the home of liberty—the enemy of tyrants—the refuge for the oppressed—the champion of republican institutions and democratic ways. . . .

With time these rather youthful and simplistic perceptions were replaced by or submerged in a third major school of thought, which we may call the Environmental or Continental. Crudely summarized, this explanation argued that "a new world makes new men." More specifically, this was the theory that Europeans were made into Americans, in part perhaps by the climate—more obviously by the topography: the raw wilderness and the empty distances—still more in the long run by the resources: by the sheer wealth in fish, furs, timber and minerals, but especially by the wealth in the soil and the vast areas of free land. So America was essentially a roomier Europe, a richer Europe, an unspoiled Europe, a far-away Europe whose virgin soil and forests would call out the best natural qualities in man, whose wealth would free us from the evil class struggle, and whose very vastness called for a federal decentralized government—to say nothing of mammoth steamboats, whopping locomotives, and a humor of exaggeration boasting some of the tallest tales ever to come down the pike. . . . Nor has it been Americans alone who have held such views. From our very beginnings (and even before) we have seemed to Europeans the Land of Plenty, the Land of Liberty, the Land of Goodness. So Europeans, too, have played with economic or political or moral revelations. . . .

[But] any one of these answers, or even all three together, were somehow insufficient to explain American character. Our colonial ancestors were not just richer, freer, or more moral Englishmen. Nor was their experience just a battle between the inheritance and the environment. Rather there had been two other factors of quite noticeable influence: the melting pot, and continued contact with Europe. So Wertenbaker [Professor Thomas Jefferson Wertenbaker, historian, author of *The First Americans*] constructed a fourfold explanation for his later books. Americans, he said, were shaped by four factors: (1) Inheritance; (2) Local conditions or the environment; (3) The Melting Pot, or the presence of other Europeans; and (4) Continued Contacts with Europe, the trade in things and ideas, especially psychic intercourse and culture borrowing. These influences one might visualize as a kind of square or quadrilateral of forces encompassing the American mystery—and they made a much broader and more satisfying picture. Especially the continued contacts. For obviously the Americans had not brought all their furniture on the Mayflower. Nor would the western exposure be the only side of our house. Nor were we entirely a self-made nation. Rather we had lived and continued to live under intermittent but heavy bombardment from Europe. Indeed it seems almost obvious that Americans have borrowed far more than they have invented, or taken from the Indians and the woods. Why? Because we began as simple and somewhat old-fashioned folk, and were slow, very slow, to become a culture center ourselves. For almost three hundred years we were "the fringe on the shawl of Europe." Most especially this fourth factor of continued contacts enables us to account for many of the novelties or peculiarities or changes in our development without calling on either geography or racial genius or intervention from on high.

Wertenbaker's four forces made a kind of square of tensions, comprehensive, neat, in balance. But perhaps the balance was too neat? Perhaps too much was still left out, or unexplained, especially the vagaries and peculiarities of our historical experience. What peculiarities or influences? After years of learning and teaching about the foreign relations of American culture, I would suggest, as a frame for thinking, that we accept Wertenbaker's quartet of forces, but add four more. I do not see how we can comprehend the American experience without these additional basic factors: (5) Accident; (6) Migration; (7) Choice; and (8) Repetition.

(5) By *Accident* I mean just that: luck, chance, the unplanned event, particularly the accidents of timing and the accumulated weight of "happenstance." Accident could be strong enough to remake the physical environment, and quite change the racial composition, as witness what happened to the colonies of Virginia and Maryland after the

introduction of tobacco. How different they would have been if Rolfe's tobacco plants, brought in from the West Indies, had *not* grown (and the colonists had had to depend on the bitter and biting North American tobacco plant called "'shag")! With no tobacco crop, no slaves either. Or again, how very different our nation and our whole national history would have been if Eli Whitney's cotton gin had not made upland or short-staple cotton profitable, and so given the slave system a second lease on life and spread it across the whole South. As Mark Twain once remarked: "Name the greatest of all inventors? Accident!"

(6) By *Migration* I mean the selective and transforming process of moving. Migration was a strong factor, strong enough to qualify the inheritance. For not all Englishmen or Europeans came over, and the experience of moving changed those that did. And they kept on moving.

(7) By *Choice* I mean purpose: the exercise of will, the deliberate perpetuation or deliberate rejection of human ingredients or social culture.

(8) Finally, by *Repetition* I mean that those efforts succeeded, those peculiarities became established, which were tried not once but often, which derived from more than one source, which were repeated through time.

My reading is that Accident, Migration, Choice and Repetition modified each of those more familiar influences of Inheritance, Environment, Melting Pot and Cultural Borrowing—all of them interacted on each other—and together they effectively shaped a New Version of Western Civilization.

How they did this is obviously too big a story to encompass in a brief essay. So perhaps the best one can do is to suggest by example. I pick just a few illustrations—arbitrarily from a great number—because these examples have interested me, and given me personally a new view of our past.

Accident

Suppose we start with *Accident*, and especially certain accidents of timing. My first illustration is the major acci-

dent that the American nation was made when Europe was
changing and advancing faster than ever before. So it was
impossible for us to keep up! Even when we started even,
we were soon old-fashioned. And atavism became one of the
hallmarks of the planting: as witness the archaisms in our
language, the more primitive skills, the old cattle and old
vegetables.

It followed that when the new European improvements
did percolate across the Atlantic they came unevenly, more
or less, sooner or later (or even not at all!). The borrowing
was slow, imperfect and incomplete; and parallel invention
did not make up. So with time the settlers came to seem
modern in some things, behind the times in many others:
"While old England is becoming young, new England is becoming old."

In the long run this might have some advantages, in
saving steps and avoiding painful trial and error. For to
invent is glorious, to adapt is profitable, but to imitate is
easiest of all. Yet suppose we later failed to borrow? Or suppose Europe changed or even destroyed itself before we took
what she had to offer? In any case, as colonies we were fated
to lag behind, and even today in some things we may not
have caught up. By the 1890s we were the largest industrial
producers in the world, but we had no chemical industry
worth noticing until World War I, when we appropriated
Germany's trade secrets. Still later the atom bomb would
be produced in this country, but not one of the scientists
who made it possible had been born or trained in the
United States. . . . For most of our history, because of too
early separation from Europe, one of the hallmarks of
Americanism has been culture lag.

Let us look next at another great accident but one of an
entirely different order: the accident that happened to the
American Indian. The Indians were conquered much more
easily than they should have been. They never put up the
resistance they ought to have. Why? It was not just a matter
of culture weakness—of weapons or organization or food
supply—or even of alcohol. The Indians' resistance was
broken first and forever by something else: by disease. It

was biological warfare crude and simple: unrecognized, un-intended, accidental but nonetheless lethal. For down the gangplanks from the white men's ships walked sickness. As described by an Army medical historian, it was "the greatest mobilization of disease and introduction to a susceptible people of which we have record." For the Europeans brought with them smallpox, measles, typhus, dysentery and malaria. Most of our ancestors must have had the pox, or developed some immunity to that killer. But the Indians hadn't; it dropped them like flies. So the redskins melted away before the feet of the white man; and the whole sav-age continent with an inexorable deliquescence became a quite different sort of place. And it hadn't been planned at all.

One could toss in the accidents of personality (or of as-sassination), and think what a difference a Washington and a Franklin (or an Aaron Burr or Abraham Lincoln) would make, but the point is sufficiently clear. National develop-ment is twisted around accidents. History is accident in print. So let us Americans not be beguiled by determinisms in looking back. We were shaped in no small part by chance.

Migration

On the other hand, there were some consistencies or complex of probabilities; and one of the greatest was *Migra-tion*. Migration—the anticipation, experience, repetition and memory of moving—exercised an enormous influence, far greater than has been generally recognized. For migra-tion was a dangerous, difficult, unpleasant, lonely business. So not everyone came. Rather migration was selective of classes, of occupation, of temperaments and cultural atti-tudes. . . .

Socially considered, the settlement of North America was remarkable for an enormous omission; no royalty, no no-bility, no aristocracy, no fixed ruling class. With insignifi-cant exceptions no great jurists, or bishops, or doctors, or scientists or artists made that voyage. The men of the great-est skills or knowledge or breeding stayed home. And for good reason: there was no compelling incentive, they were already successful. This forced those who did come to depend on themselves. The settlement of America "shifted the emphasis from nobility to ability," we say? Perhaps. Yet the immediate result was a decapitated society—with some from the upper middle class, and many more from the lower middle class and the poor. We started with no aristocracy, no leisure class and few leisure-class arts; and the harsh demands of the wilderness fast diminished the leisurely habits of the survivors. At the same time the vast opportunities of the continent helped lift the bottom group into property owners too. So Americans grew into one big hard-working middle class—as Tocqueville was to discover—a society without head and almost (slavery excepted) without feet. "God made America for the poor." "In America," said a Frenchman, "all that has disappeared which with us is lowly."

Another result was a thinner, narrower, shallower society —deficient in music, theatre and the fine arts—with no professional schools anywhere and few specialized men before the Revolution. The fine flower of specialization was not appreciated or cultivated. We became jacks of all trades and masters of none. Even our churches fell into the hands of laymen, while our colleges were administered by amateurs. The common law was vulgarized; our language, the same. For the sculptors we had "cunning carvers," and for architects "the serviceable carpenter." To repeat, our colonial societies, because of migration, were in many ways limited or defective—and the later waves of migration helped hardly at all. So we learned to do without. . . .

Choice

This points to the factor of *Choice* or deliberate selection. Much of culture-carrying and of culture-borrowing was of course automatic, unconscious or taken for granted. But some was not. Can there be free will in culture? I believe there can—or at least such exercise of will, such defiance of man and nature, such lunk-headed persistence as amounts to the same thing. The "New Version" of Europe was not just the blind consequence of accident and migration, of inheritance and mixture and adaptation, but elements of it were deliberately, almost wilfully willed into being. Let us look back just a moment at the deliberate planting of "the Lord's Vineyard of New England."

The first desideratum or moral imperative for the settlers of Massachusetts Bay was a purified religion—the rule of the Saints—a new and better Church. The second was a new and better Commonwealth, by magistrates and town meetings and government by the Freeman. And the third, as [the historian] S. E. Morison . . . so eloquently demonstrated, was an intellectual system—with a printing press and the publication of religious books and poetry and newspapers and even scientific observations long generations before the Virginians or the French in Canada lifted themselves to such a level. Also a school system from dame school to fifty-family common schools to hundred-family grammar schools to a college out in the cow country in Newtown (which they renamed Cambridge). And for this college they appropriated four hundred pounds and the avails of the Charlestown Ferry (a breath-taking sacrifice), and solicited contributions of "college corn" from all over New England for free scholarships! At first the standards could not be too high, but clearly it was "the best thing New England ever thought upon." And later in Connecticut they would do it again. In defiance of poverty and the raw continent.

The Puritans "took thought" or exercised choice also in some negative ways. They excluded pagan holidays, pagan music and musical instruments in worship, and what they regarded as the most sinful, theatre—though in so doing they were depriving themselves and their children of much that the Elizabethans had been best at! Their exclusiveness even went beyond religion, for they were no more anxious to receive foreigners or vagabonds than Baptists or Quakers. Such undesirables they deported or forced to move on. So New England came to be peopled overwhelmingly with their own kind: the achievement of character by omission.

As a result of such deliberate insistences and deliberate exclusions there developed a homogeneous, intelligent, community-minded, disciplined people with a driving faith. How else account for their influence later in our nation? . . .

Nor would exclusiveness shape only New England; it would later give character also to the South. When was the "Old South" most separate and distinct? In the Colonial period? Hardly. It had the climate and crops and slave system but not the people: anybody and everybody settled in the South. No. It's character was hardened in the years 1815-1860: when slavery became unpopular elsewhere, when immigrants were reluctant to move in, when southerners became conscious of their "peculiar institution" and conscious they were losing power. Then they deliberately came together to build and perpetuate, this time a quite different kingdom, the Cotton Kingdom. And where they might have had factories and mills they preferred to stay planters; where they might have built railroads they stuck to mules; where they might have cultivated science they clung to the Bible; and where they might have studied Mill, they reread Walter Scott. One can invite any skeptic and any materialist to examine the wilful manufacture of the "Old South."

Another great example of the exercise of Choice in nation-building has been the rejection of aristocracy in this country. This rejection was in part accidental, in part obviously circumstantial, but it was also deliberate. In fact it is fascinating to notice how, not just once but over and over, this American branch of European society has thrown over, or got out from under, or disestablished *authority*. I'm referring not just to aristocracy of blood but also to aristocracies and authorities of many kinds, from privileges of wealth or of occupation to priorities of arrival or superiorities of learning. . . .

Repetition

The last point I should like to make . . . [is] the importance of *Repetition*. For it seems that in the American experience no trait or characteristic or peculiarity gets established by just one happening and no strong institution derives from a single source. For example, what made the suspicion and even hatred of England endemic in nineteenth century America was not just colonial misrule, with the Stamp Act and the Revolutionary experience, but the strug

gle for the fisheries, free seas, and freedom from impress-
ment, followed by the Northwest Posts dispute and the
Indian menace, then the War of 1812, and then the arrival
of the Catholic Irish! By contrast, the French in 1778-1793
enjoyed an enormous vogue; but then came the excesses of
the Revolution and Napoleon—the contacts were broken—
and French influence just fades out of the American picture.
Even Lafayette would have been forgotten, perhaps, if he
had not come back in 1824-1825 and made a long, emotional, and highly publicized trip through the back country.
Villages were now named after him, his descendants were
granted citizenship, and it is said that his trip achieved
more space in our school books than did his role in the
War of Independence. So was created the Lafayette legend
—and it was *Echo* that did the trick.

Perhaps the echo with the longest reverberation that we
have known has been immigration. For we came not once or
even three times, but repeatedly and almost continuously for
more than 350 years. All of us began as immigrants, and
not a generation has passed without some fresh infusion of
refugees and optimists and ethnic groups, carrying with
them their wounds and ambitions and ambivalences about
the countries they had left behind. So if today one would
understand the "gut" reactions of the American voter, one
could do worse than to think of the immigrant under his
skin.

If I should be allowed only a single illustration of the
echo-effect, I would cite the Idea of 1776. How did the
Americans reach the discovery, so brilliantly stated by
Thomas Jefferson in the Declaration of Independence, that
when men felt oppressed, the social compact had been violated and the people had a natural right, not to change
Kings, but to form a new compact of government? The answer is that they had been taught to do their own reading
in the Bible, and so had encountered the idea of covenant.
Again the Common Law protected the rights of individuals
or at least of Englishmen. They had read Milton on Kings
and Magistrates, and learned from the Revolution of 1688.
Locke's compact theory of government had been absorbed

and taught in the colonial colleges; while Montesquieu and Blackstone were looked to by the lawyer-politicians. So they had met that idea, that theory, again and again in print.

But the idea of contract and of a compact of government came right out of their personal experience, too. The original Company charters had been contracts. They had traded by contract. The Mayflower Compact, the Fundamental Articles of Connecticut, the Articles of Agreement of the Providence Plantations had been compacts of government. And the town meetings and the church covenants were self-made self-governments on a miniature scale. . . .

Accident—Migration—Choice—Repetition. These help me to explain to myself why that old and simple equation—the adaptation of English ways to a new continent—somehow, indeed almost invariably, fails to explain. For it wasn't average Englishmen or Europeans who came over; and their exposure to the continent was in some ways less trying than the psychological choices they had had to make. . . .

Americanism has been difficult to invent because it had to be put together out of omissions and exaggerations, anticipations and postponements, accidents, reinfusions and contradictions without number. Perhaps we may conclude that the 1776 American version of Europe was therefore not so much the product of invention, or even of adaptation, as of some things else. Because of accident, migration, choice, repetition, a new combination was in the making. America was Europe—but in a different proportion.

OF OUR SPIRITUAL STRIVINGS [3]

Between me and the other world there is ever an unasked question: unasked by some through feelings of delicacy; by others through the difficulty of rightly framing it. All, nevertheless, flutter round it. They approach me in a half-hesitant sort of way, eye me curiously or compassionately, and then, instead of saying directly, How does it feel to be a problem? they say, I know an excellent colored man

[3] From Chapter 1 of *The Souls of Black Folk*, by W. E. B. Du Bois, noted educator and writer (1868-1963). Fawcett. '61. p 15–17. This work was first published in 1903.

in my town; or, I fought at Mechanicsville; or, Do not these Southern outrages make your blood boil? At these I smile, or am interested, or reduce the boiling to a simmer, as the occasion may require. To the real question, How does it feel to be a problem? I answer seldom a word.

And yet, being a problem is a strange experience—peculiar even for one who has never been anything else, save perhaps in babyhood and in Europe. It is in the early days of rollicking boyhood that the revelation first bursts upon one, all in a day, as it were. I remember well when the shadow swept across me. I was a little thing, away up in the hills of New England, where the dark Housatonic winds between Hoosac and Taghkanic to the sea. In a wee wooden schoolhouse, something put it into the boys' and girls' heads to buy gorgeous visiting-cards—ten cents a package—and exchange. The exchange was merry, till one girl, a tall newcomer, refused my card—refused it peremptorily, with a glance. Then it dawned upon me with a certain suddenness that I was different from the others; or like, mayhap, in heart and life and longing, but shut out from their world by a vast veil. I had thereafter no desire to tear down that veil, to creep through; I held all beyond it in common contempt, and lived above it in a region of blue sky and great wandering shadows. That sky was bluest when I could beat my mates at examination-time, or beat them at a foot-race, or even beat their stringy heads. Alas, with the years all this fine contempt began to fade; for the worlds I longed for, and all their dazzling opportunities, were theirs, not mine. But they should not keep these prizes, I said; some, all, I would wrest from them. Just how I would do it I could never decide: by reading law, by healing the sick, by telling the wonderful tales that swam in my head—some way. With other black boys the strife was not so fiercely sunny: their youth shrunk into tasteless sycophancy, or into silent hatred of the pale world about them and mocking distrust of everything white; or wasted itself in bitter cry, Why did God make me an outcast and a stranger in mine own house? The shades of the prison-house closed round about us all: walls strait and stubborn to the whitest, but relentlessly narrow, tall, and unscalable to sons of night who must plod darkly on in resignation, or beat unavailing palms against the stone, or steadily, half hopelessly, watch the streak of blue above.

After the Egyptian and Indian, the Greek and Roman, the Teuton and Mongolian, the Negro is a sort of seventh son, born with a veil, and gifted with second-sight in this American world—a world which yields him no true self-consciousness, but only lets him see himself through the revelation of the other world. It is a peculiar sensation, this double-consciousness, this sense of always looking at one's self through the eyes of others, of measuring one's soul by the tape of a world that looks on in amused contempt and pity. One ever feels his twoness—an American, a Negro; two souls, two thoughts, two unreconciled strivings; two warring ideals in one dark body, whose dogged strength alone keeps it from being torn asunder.

The history of the American Negro is the history of this strife—this longing to attain self-conscious manhood, to merge his double self into a better and truer self. In this merging he wishes neither of the older selves to be lost. He would not Africanize America, for America has too much to teach the world and Africa. He would not bleach his Negro soul in a flood of white Americanism, for he knows that Negro blood has a message for the world. He simply wishes to make it possible for a man to be both a Negro and an American, without being cursed and spit upon by his fellows, without having the doors of Opportunity closed roughly in his face.

II. E PLURIBUS

EDITOR'S INTRODUCTION

E Pluribus Unum: from many, one—our national motto,
on our coins and paper currency. When it was adopted, in
the eighteenth century, it referred to the political union of
thirteen separate British colonies. What does it really mean
in the last quarter of the twentieth century? Despite the
controversy surrounding the issue of illegal immigrants, the
heyday of immigration is well behind us. Yet our multiple
cultural and racial origins are more noticeable than ever.
At least, we are talking about them more—and more pub-
licly, too. The articles in this section scan a few of the
"many" ethnic groups that constitute the American "one"
and focus on some experiences shared by a number of them.

The most universal experience, of course, was immigration. For most it was itself a traumatic experience of varying degrees of discomfort and deprivation, and it was followed by a lengthy period of adjustment, economic hard-
ship, and discrimination. But one immigrant group was
exempt from these disabilities—those most similar in race,
culture, and religion to the earliest colonists, most of whom
were white, Anglo-Saxon, and Protestant. Those WASPs
who did not call England "mother" hailed from other lands
of northern and western Europe. Retaining only a hint of
their heritages in a Dutch, French, or German name, the
white Protestant majority considers its immigrant past as
ancient family history, the ancestral struggle to adjust to a
new land lost in the mists of time. It is worth noting that,
for many such immigrants, a crucial aspect of the usual pattern was reversed: Most other immigrant groups left lands
where they—Africans, Irish Catholics, Italians, Chinese—
shared the majority culture and religion and came to America in which their differences made them conspicuous. But
the Puritans, Huguenots, Quakers and other dissenting Eu-

ropean Protestants left places where their religious radicalism made them a minority and came to an America where they settled in close proximity to other similarly dissenting Protestants.

The British, in particular, have always been right at home in America, and those coming over seem to view it as still an outpost of their country of origin. As Howard B. Furer has noted in *The British in America 1578-1970,* "the economic and social adjustments of these peoples are and have been relatively so easy that they can and have entered into American affairs as equals of the natives of this country. In addition, we may say that, in a sense, British-Americans have had no 'second generation,' no ill-adjusted class, like the children of less fortunate foreigners."

The first article in this section is a review of a new addition to the growing literature on how it feels to be a WASP in a nation of ethnics. In his review, Richard E. Lingeman also communicates his own experience as a member of a dominant group that these days is no longer so secure about itself as it used to be.

In many ways, the experiences of the Jews of Eastern Europe who emigrated to the United States in vast numbers from the 1880s to the 1920s were prototypic. In his introduction to the book called *A Bintel Brief* ("A Bundle of Letters"), Isaac Metzker briefly tells the story of their lives and problems as poverty-stricken newcomers—greenhorns or "greenies." It is a universal story, different perhaps in some details but not in overall impact, from the experiences of other non-WASP Europeans who arrived here in that period. The significance of *A Bintel Brief,* and its reasons for being, are explained in Metzker's essay. Also reprinted are letters from this book, each revealing an area of conflict—familiar to all groups—between the traditional, or ethnic lifestyle and that of the new world, as demonstrated in the differences between the generations.

The problems faced by eastern and southern European immigrants, however, pale by comparison with the hurdle that awaited those whose crossing was over the Pacific Ocean rather than the Atlantic. Chinese and Japanese laborer were literally imported by American employers. This produced a very special immigrant group indeed—exclusively male and young—and one that encountered extreme racial discrimination as well as miserably low pay ("coolie" wages). Clustering in their Chinatowns in cities, first on the West Coast and then across the country, the Asian immigrants often remained in their enclaves long after they achieved middle-class prosperity because they were unable to rent or buy suitable housing in other communities.

In 1970 there were 591,000 Japanese, 435,000 Chinese, and 343,000 Filipinos living in the United States. There was also a sizeable Korean population—66,000. Almost all were urban dwellers, and most lived in the western states—especially Hawaii and California—and in New York, Illinois, and Massachusetts.

In the 1970s America's Asian population has grown considerably. Increased numbers of Japanese, Chinese, and Filipinos have continued to arrive, and their ranks have been swelled by Thai and Vietnamese refugees. These, like the others, tend to settle on the West Coast, although New York City has an expanding Thai population and Washington, D.C., and neighboring Virginia are host to many Vietnamese.

In very different circumstances are the vast numbers of resident alien Japanese, located mainly in New York City and California and changing the character of the neighborhoods and even of the cities in which they live. Most of them, here temporarily as relatively affluent employees of Japanese companies with branches in this country, will undoubtedly return home; but some will remain, and those who leave will be replaced, creating a predictable continuing influence.

American receptivity to these groups in recent years is a far cry from such discriminatory practices of earlier years as restrictive immigration policies and laws preventing interracial marriage (it was not until June 12, 1967, that the Supreme Court ruled that states could not prohibit marriage between white and nonwhite persons). American xenophobia reached its nadir during World War II, with the forced removal of thousands of Americans of Japanese descent from their homes and jobs to hastily established relocation centers or camps.

Stereotyping—the pidgin-English-speaking Asian servants in Hollywood films, "humorous" verse about "the heathen Chinee," and the caricatured "Jap" in the posters and comic strips of the 1940s—was endemic, and there was little factual information to serve as a corrective. In the late 1960s an analysis of literature dealing with Chinese-Americans over the last half century found that it consisted primarily of the same pejorative stereotypes, with no serious work or accurate data.

Reprinted here is one article that indicates several levels of the problems faced by Asian-Americans. In it, Emma Gee tells the story of the first generation of women to come here from Asia. They came as brides, often to husbands they had never met, to a strange world where the customs and security of their traditional tightly knit society no longer existed.

In the next article the focus shifts to ethnicity in the present—how it is expressed and maintained. Murray Schumach describes the environment created in one of New York City's many ethnic neighborhoods, this one a Greek-American community in the borough of Queens. The multiethnic character of the city was underscored on the day this article appeared in the New York *Times:* not only were there the usual advertisements for restaurants of every national persuasion, but there were also announcements of a Yiddish Film Festival and a Himalayan Harvest Festival.

Constituting a very large segment of the population are 11.1 million Americans of Hispanic or Latino origin with ethnic ties to several countries in the Western Hemisphere as well as to Spain. Mexican-Americans, or Chicanos, with 6.5 million, are the second largest ethnic minority in the United States. Central and South America are the source of 752,000; Cuba, with 687,000, represents nearly as large a component; Puerto Rico is the source of 1.7 million, and all other Hispanic nations combined add another 1.3 million. Each of the many Hispanic-American groups brings with it a different cultural heritage and immigrant exper ence. While the names and language may be the same, and some of the problems may be similar, the ethnic heritages of Mexican-Americans, Cuban-Americans, Puerto Ricans, Spanish-Americans, Portuguese-Americans and other Latinos are quite distinct. The unique Mexican heritage of the Chicanos blends both the Hispanic and Indian traditions.

The Mexican influence on the rest of North America dates back to millennia before the arrival of the conquistadores. Agriculture in the New World was a Mexican invention; and the cultivation of corn—and later of beans and squash—learned through Mexican contacts made possible the development of the Pueblo Indian culture in what is now the southwestern United States. From ancient times Mexican crafts have been transmitted to American Indian cultures, among them leather working, pottery making, and silversmithing. The Spanish conquest in the sixteenth century superimposed a new influence, but the old ways remained (and even today more than 10 percent of Mexican people use a native language as their mother tongue).

The long period of Mexican influence on and immigration to the land north and west of the Rio Grande, the issues being confronted by today's Mexican-Americans, and their new spirit and organization to preserve their cultural traditions and achieve economic progress—a movement known as Chicanismo—are the subject of a report by ethnohistorian Jack D. Forbes, the fifth selection in this section.

The next excerpt, taken from a pamphlet issued by the Institute on Pluralism and Group Identity of the American Jewish Committee, focuses on the process of "moving up" as it works to change social and economic relationships. Then, in the final article, Andrew M. Greeley, one of the most provocative observers of the ethnic scene, surveys the sociological import of our uniquely multiethnic nation. He points up the relative lack so far of serious research in ethnic studies by social scientists and the need for such studies as steps toward the practical solution of real social, economic, and political problems of modern society.

"EVERYONE ELSE IS AN ETHNIC" [1]

I suppose I qualify as a WASP under Florence King's definition: German on my father's side, English on my mother's, but the trans-Atlantic business took place well over one hundred years ago. White. Sufficiently Protestant to know the words to "Jesus Loves Me" and "There Is Sunshine in My Soul Today."

Being a WASP means that everyone else is an ethnic, which is why WASP's end up either as bigots or so fearful of offending they can't even call someone a Jew without lowering their voice and smiling. WASP's were able to set up invidious ethnic distinctions only because they arrived here first; it took some chutzpah (or is that word *challah?*) to make the Indians, who were really here first, a minority group—not to mention the blacks, who were extradited here, then given WASP names as consolation.

Now, history has had its revenge; WASP's still own all the money and most of the country clubs, but nobody pays them any attention. Ethnicism and roots are in; WASP's are the invisible ethnics. WASP's have, of course, been tracing their roots for years, but none of the spinster aunts upon whom the task devolved ever thought of writing a best seller about the process; and who, besides the local chapter of the Daughters of the American Revolution or genealogical society, would have been interested?

Envy for the Ethnics

Nowadays, says Florence King, WASP's pay the ethnics the secret tribute of envy ("So warm," "colorful," "family oriented"), often employing stereotypes originally devised for purposes of prejudice. WASP's used to have big families too, which sociologists have since dismissed with the term "economic units"; they were part of the WASP's burden of conquering the continent (with the help of a few black slaves, Irish laborers, Swedish farmers, Italian construction workers, etc.). After they had subdivided the real estate and

[1] From review by staff editor and reviewer Richard R. Lingeman of Florence King's *WASP, Where Is Thy Sting?* New York *Times.* p C 17. Je. 30, '77. © 1977 by The New York Times Company. Reprinted by permission.

made a fortune, the wealthier WASP's took up birth control. At any rate, what with all that hard work and Puri-
tanism too, it's no wonder WASP's have less fun.

In *WASP, Where Is Thy Sting?* Florence King has gathered together a lot of the standard WASP traits, crotchets and
behavior patterns. Because we're not interesting, she seems
to be saying, she will show how funny we are. It is a sound
approach. One of her techniques is to create comic types, like
Mrs. Jonesborough, the upper-class WASP wife in the suburbs who's always improving herself for her husband (who's
always away in some Holiday Inn or another on business);
she must decide whether she should "sweep the floor or
exercise her vaginal muscles." She is a lousy cook who in the
middle of Happy Hour groans, "Oh, God!" and rushes to
the kitchen to dump some canned peaches into the Jell-O
mold.

Then you'll remember Todd Armstrong, class of 195–, a
straight-C man who preferred girls with a "C-plus libido"
so he wouldn't have a pregnancy on his hands that would
louse up his career. The girl of his dreams was Mary Beth
Butterfield, full of school spirit and always smiling. She
majored in "Soc" and had a photographic memory, which
enabled her to get good grades on objective-question quizzes
despite a furious semester of extracurricular good works.
Say "Sartre" to her and she would immediately reply,
"Ummm, existentialism."

A Lot of Home Truths

At times Miss King is too jokey, or else playing varia-
tions of the old "In-Out," "Upper-middle-lower-brow"
games, but she also manages to hit upon a lot of home
truths. She is hilarious about the kind of WASP mother
who raises her sons to be tough and unsissyish, all the while
weaving about them an Oedipal web tighter than Mrs.
Portnoy could ever dream of. The result is the avowed
hetero son, who marries late, calls his mother by her first
name and gets into cat-fights with her as she orders a fourth
martini at the country club: "Do you really think you
should, Babs? You've had enough." When he marries, he

absolutely adores his mother-in-law, if she is chic, and soon
the two "are *ciao*-ing each other and swapping catty criticisms about the way Jackie Onassis wears her hunt derby."

On sex, Miss King echoes D. H. Lawrence on the
WASP's predilection for violence and repressiveness. Mur-
der is "oneness acting alone to end troublesome emotional
entanglements. It goes without saying that the murderer
does not need people. The sensualist does. Thus sex threat-
ens self-sufficiency as a good clean kill preserves it." Although she commits Mad Avenuese such as "We are not
'people people,'" she follows up with the insight that "close
emotional contact with our own species presents too many
threats."

LETTERS TO THE EDITOR: THE JEWISH EXPERIENCE [2]

Introduction

In 1880 when America had a population of fifty million,
one quarter of a million of that total were Jews. The majority
of these Jews were German and Sephardic who had come here
with the languages of the countries in which their families
had lived for generations. The new immigrants whose
mother tongue was Yiddish were at that time in the minority.

The mass immigration of the Yiddish-speaking Jews from
eastern Europe started in the early 1880s. They were fleeing
from the bloody pogroms in Russia and Rumania and from
poverty and persecution in other eastern European countries.

The mass immigration of Jews to the United States was
like the wandering of peoples in ancient times and it seemed
for a time that some of the eastern European countries
would be completely drained of their Jewish populations.
The situation might possibly have come to that point, in

    [2] From *A Bintel Brief,* compiled and edited by Isaac Metzker, longtime editor
and contributor to the *Jewish Daily Forward,* author of several novels in Yiddish. *A Bintel Brief.* Doubleday. '71. p 7–17, 158–9, 163–4, 211–13. Copyright © 1971 by Isaac Metzker. Used by permission of Doubleday & Company,
Inc.

fact, had it not been for the passage of strict quota laws at the beginning of the 1920s which all but closed the gates of America to these immigrants.

From 1881 to 1925, however, 2.65 million Jewish immigrants managed to come to America from eastern European countries alone. At that time this total amounted to a third of the Jewish population of all of eastern Europe.

Wonderful tales had come from remote America to the Jews in eastern Europe, even to the most far-flung towns and villages where no railways ran. Such magic words as *Golden Land, Freedom, Equality,* had animated them—somewhere, across the great ocean, a new land was being built, founded on freedom and equality for all people, a refuge for all who were suffering and persecuted.

For the impoverished and tormented Jews, these tales seemed the fulfillment of their dreams of finding a haven for themselves and their families, a place somewhere under the sun where they could have peace and live like human beings. These dreams and the tales they heard gave them the courage to set out for this country on the long quest for freedom and bread. They plodded along Europe's paths and roads, stole across borders in the dark of night, traveled by horse and wagon and train, endured a long painful voyage across the stormy ocean.

On the American shores, near Ellis Island, the Goddess of Freedom held high the bright torch for the immigrants. She enticed them with promises and stimulated their imagination. Many of them believed that as soon as they disembarked from the boat they would find heaven on earth and an end to all their suffering. But they were to experience many bitter disappointments in the new land.

In those years when new Jewish immigrants were arriving daily from eastern Europe, committees were formed among the Jews already settled to encourage the newcomers to go west. But a great many of them preferred to remain near the shore where they had left the ship. They settled in the old tenements of New York, primarily in a small area of the lower East Side. There, crowded together, they stayed near *landsleit* [compatriots or fellow townspeople] who had migrated before them, or near friends who had come on the same boat.

It did not take them long to find out that no luxuries awaited them—that one had to struggle hard here for the necessities of life. The transition from their old way of life in the *shtetel* [small town or village] to a new life in the seething, vast city of New York was not an easy one to make. Back home, everything had been founded on traditional Judaism. There the Sabbath was sacred. Even an unbeliever would not dare desecrate the Sabbath in public. *Kashruth* [dietary laws observed by traditional Jews] was carefully observed; the Jewish holidays were properly celebrated. Even few "enlightened" men in small towns would dare to trim or shave their beards.

Thus had the Jews conducted themselves within strong traditions for generations and generations. Now, suddenly, they were thrust into a totally different world where they found it necessary to break with tradition and flout time-honored laws. They went to work on the Sabbath, they shaved their beards, and many of them began to eat non-*kosher* foods.

The "green" years were difficult and full of problems for the immigrants. Thousands and thousands of them were drawn into the needle trades and many found other types of employment. Working men and women at that time were not yet organized, and the majority of them were terribly exploited by their bosses. These were the days of the real "sweatshop" system. Not only the adults but children too worked under the worst conceivable conditions . . . often seven days a week, twelve and even fourteen hours a day, and for miserable wages. The immigrants lived in poverty, crowded in small damp rooms without daylight or fresh air. In the summer it was hard to breathe in the tenements and during the stifling nights they often slept by the thousands on the roofs.

Not only did they usually work for meager wages, but during slack times there were no jobs at any wage. Unemployment lasted for long periods of time. The immigrants often lacked the money to make the all-important payment on a steamship ticket purchased on the installment plan for someone else in the family waiting to immigrate. There was no bread, milk or money for rent.

During depression periods it was not uncommon to see families huddled on the sidewalks with their meager household effects. They had been thrown out of their apartments by the landlords because they were behind in their rent payments. Often, a plate was placed for collecting rent money near a haggard mother who sat with her little children on their bedding. Neighbors and passers-by who were moved by the scene threw coins in the dish. A few dollars might accumulate by the end of the day, and toward evening a neighbor would take the small sum to the landlord, who would let the family back into their apartment.

In those years of mass immigration there was much to be deplored in this country, most specifically in the great city of New York. Countless wrongs were committed against the new immigrants, many of which even violated the principles of the United States Constitution. The poverty was oppressive, and more than one newcomer was driven to suicide.

Nevertheless, the majority of the immigrants refused to give up their dreams. They would not, they could not. The visions that had accompanied them to the new land persisted.

Within them raged a protest against all that was evil here but they seemed to sense a promised freedom in the air and did not lose faith. They still believed that things could be good for them in the "Golden Land" and spoke with assurance about the good life awaiting their children. They knew that they had not come here as invaders, forcing their way into a country already built up and populated by a people for generations. And their awareness that they had come with the same rights as the many other immigrants of various nationalities who had settled here and begun to build a new, richer life bolstered their courage. They were young and energetic and would not be easily discouraged. They were determined to make this country their home.

* * *

The [Jewish Daily] *Forward*, a Yiddish daily newspaper in America which celebrated its seventieth anniversary in 1967, played an important role in helping the eastern European Jewish immigrants transplant and adjust themselves to American life. . . .

Primarily a workingman's newspaper, [it] attracted many of the immigrants who had become shopworkers. The paper began to teach them about trade unionism. It explained in their mother tongue how important it was for them to be organized, to unite to fight for higher wages, shorter working hours and decent treatment by the bosses. And the newcomers, who were lonely here, clung to the *Forward* in turn as to a newfound friend. It became their teacher and guide. The newspaper concerned itself with their lot, spoke to their hearts and quickly gained their respect and confidence.

It is no exaggeration to say that the pages of the *Forward* over the seven decades contain a true epical history of the Jewish mass immigration and the immigrants' adaptation to life in this country. The saga of their struggles, achievements and contributions to the country were written into the day-by-day news. All sorts of articles, literary novels, sketches and special features were printed in this newspaper. One of these features . . . was and still is the "Bintel Brief" [a bundle of letters, a mailbag].

Abraham Cahan was, except for a brief interval, the editor of the newspaper from its founding until shortly before his death in 1951. He maintained that the *Forward* should not devote itself exclusively to trade unionism, to political and social problems. From the outset, he broadened the interests of the paper and enlivened it with varied reading material, including light articles dealing with daily life. The daily newspaper thus drew readers from all strata and classes. . . .

Mr. Cahan, who became well known as a talented author with his novel, *The Rise of David Levinsky,* and other works, was a strong advocate of realism. He not only printed realistic stories by well-known writers but made an effort to bring the reality of Jewish life in America into his newspaper. Through light articles he inspired and encouraged the readers to write to the *Forward* about any unusual events in their own lives, and about their own problems. Mr. Cahan firmly believed that "truth is stranger than fiction," and as far back as 1903 planned a special feature for the newspaper in which the readers could express themselves, a section of the paper which would mirror real life. As a result, the daily feature, "A Bintel Brief," was established in 1906. It immediately became very popular and is still, to this day, a most important feature of the paper.

The first three letters were printed with an introduction by the editor on January 20, 1906. One of the letters, written by a woman, gives us an insight into the poverty in which the immigrant working-class families lived on the lower East Side. The woman had a sick husband, and their eldest son was the breadwinner of the family. The son wanted very much to own a watch and chain, the sort that were then being worn across the front of the vest. For a long time he saved from his lunch money until he was able to buy himself the watch. But it seems the watch lay hidden in the dresser most of the time and, according to the woman's letter, it became their security against poverty. Since they could never save a dollar and lived from hand to mouth, every time "slack season" came, she took the watch to the pawnshop. For the few dollars she got there, they were able to live through a period in which there was no work.

Suddenly the watch disappeared. Her son was unemployed and she wanted to take the watch to the pawnshop but couldn't find it. She suspected that a poor neighbor of hers, who came to the house quite often and was also jobless, had been driven by her own need to take her son's watch to pawn. Since it was embarrassing to discuss the matter personally with the neighbor, the woman appealed to her through the *Forward* to send her the pawn ticket in the mail. She assured her neighbor, in the letter, that she would never reproach her because she knew her condition only too well, and added that they would remain friends.

The feature, "A Bintel Brief," caught on quickly. For many readers the letters awakened a desire to unburden their hearts, to reveal their own problems and ask for ad-

vice. Whole sacks of mail began to pour in. Often the daily
column contained several letters. . . .

As time went on, the subject matter of the letters changed
and continued to change a great deal.

The majority of the present-day letter writers have now
been in the country for many years, and they are no longer
young. Many of them are now retired; they are well established here, with children and grandchildren. The problems they now write about to the "Bintel Brief" deal mainly
with family matters. . . .

Many of the letter writers today are old readers of the
Forward and their close ties to the newspaper, as well as
their confidence in the editor of the "Bintel Brief," have
grown stronger and deeper over the years. They often express their trust with an opening remark like: "You are the
only one whom I can trust and to whom I can pour out my
heart . . ." "As a reader of the *Forverts* since 1910, when
the big cloakmakers' strike took place, I appeal to you for
advice, and I will do as you tell me . . ." "I know that no
one can advise me as well as you can." One reader writes
that his asking for an opinion and counsel from the editor
reminds him of the way people went to the *rebbe* [the village wise man, learned in the traditional law, dispenser of
advice on all subjects] in the old country.

The editor who answers the letters is far removed from
the role of the *rebbe* (who gave people not only advice but
blessings and amulets too). But, in his answers to the letters,
the editor is more than just an adviser who gives perfunctory
counsel. He is also the teacher and the preacher, and often
his answer to a letter turns into an instructive lecture.

Letters

Worthy Editor,

I am sure that the problem I'm writing about affects
many Jewish homes. It deals with immigrant parents and
their American-born children.

My parents, who have been readers of your paper for
years, came from Europe. They have been here in this coun-

try over thirty years and were married twenty-eight years ago. They have five sons, and I am one of them. The oldest of us is twenty-seven and the youngest twenty-one.

We are all making a decent living. One of us works for the State Department. A second is a manager in a large store, two are in business, and the youngest is studying law. Our parents do not need our help because my father has a good job.

We, the five brothers, always speak English to each other. Our parents know English too, but they speak only Yiddish, not just among themselves but to us too, and even to our American friends who come to visit us. We beg them not to speak Yiddish in the presence of our friends, since they can speak English, but they don't want to. It's a sort of stubbornness on their part, and a great deal of quarreling goes on between our parents and ourselves because of it.

Their answer is: "Children, we ask you not to try to teach us how to talk to people. We are older than you."

Imagine, even when we go with our father to buy something in a store on Fifth Avenue, New York, he insists on speaking Yiddish. We are not ashamed of our parents, God forbid, but they ought to know where it's proper and where it's not. If they talk Yiddish among themselves at home, or to us, it's bad enough, but among strangers and Christians? Is that nice? It looks as if they're doing it to spite us. Petty spats grow out of it. They want to keep only to their old ways and don't want to take up our new ways.

We beg you, friend Editor, to express your opinion on this question, and if possible send us your answer in English, because we can't read Yiddish.

Accept our thanks for your answer, which we expect soon,

> Respectfully,
> I. and the Four Brothers
> (1933)

ANSWER:
We see absolutely no crime in the parents' speaking Yiddish

to their sons. The Yiddish language is dear to them and they want to speak in that language to their children and all who understand it. It may also be that they are ashamed to speak their imperfect English among strangers so they prefer to use their mother tongue.

From the letter, we get the impression that the parents are not fanatics, and with their speaking Yiddish they are not out to spite the children. But it would certainly not be wrong if the parents were to speak English too, to the children. People should and must learn the language of their country.

Dear Editor,

I come to you with my family problem because I think you are the only one who can give me practical advice. I am a man in my fifties, and I came to America when I was very young. I don't have to tell you how hard life was for a "greenhorn" in those times. I suffered plenty. But that didn't keep me from falling in love with a girl from my home town and marrying her.

I harnessed myself to the wagon of family life and pulled with all my strength. My wife was faithful and she gave me a hand in pulling the wagon. The years flew fast and before we looked around we were parents of four children who brightened and sweetened our lives.

The children were dear and smart and we gave them an education that was more than we could afford. They went to college, became professionals, and are well established.

Suddenly I feel as if the floor has collapsed under my feet. I don't know how to express it, but the fact that my children are well educated and have outgrown me makes me feel bad. I can't talk to them about my problems and they can't talk to me about theirs. It's as if there were a deep abyss that divides us.

People envy me my good, fine, educated children but (I am ashamed to admit it) I often think it might be better for me if they were not so well educated, but ordinary workingmen, like me. Then we would have more in common. I have no education, because my parents were poor, and in the old country they couldn't give me the opportunities that I could give my children. Here, in America, I didn't have time and my mind wasn't on learning in the early years when I had to work hard.

That is my problem. I want to hear your opinion about it. I enclose my full name and address, but please do not print it. I will sign as,

Disappointed
(1938)

ANSWER:
It is truly a pleasure to have such children, and the father can really be envied. But he must not feel he has nothing in common with them any longer, because they have more education than he. There should be no chasm between father and children, and if there is, perhaps he himself created it.

In thousands of Jewish immigrant homes such educated children have grown up, and many of them remain close to their parents. Also there is no reason why the writer of this letter shouldn't be able to talk to his fine, good children about various problems, even though they are professionals and have outdistanced him in their education.

Dear Editor,
I have often read the "Bintel Brief" to learn how you have suggested solutions for the problems of your readers. Now, I would like to tell you my problem. It is difficult for me to write Yiddish so I am writing to you in English. I am a young man twenty years of age. My grandparents brought a precious heritage of *Yiddishkeit* [the culture and lifestyle of Yiddish-speaking Jews] from eastern Europe. I remember the good Jewish life they lived. I still remember how they used to sing Jewish songs, speak Yiddish, and prepare delicious *kosher* meals for my parents and me on Friday evenings. These were the best days I have yet known.

However, several years ago my grandparents passed away.

My parents and I now reside in the suburbs in an area which lacks the Jewish traditions and customs that I knew as a child. Very few except the older Jewish people in my neighborhood speak Yiddish. Few keep strictly *kosher* homes, few people observe our wonderful Sabbath in the traditional manner. Most of the young ladies I meet are not the type of Jewish girl I would like. I feel like a stranger among the Jewish girls who are interested only in rock 'n' roll and wear mini skirts. I long for the days I knew as a young boy.

Many aspects of life in this area seem to snuff out whatever remains of our beloved *Yiddishkeit*. I have recently graduated from a local university and am now starting to attend law school in a larger city. Most of the young people who will be studying there with me will not be Jewish or will be the type of Jew who does not live as one. Most of the people I will come in contact with will not have the same interests I have.

I want to know how my family and I can perpetuate our traditions. I would also like to know where I can find people of my age to share my interests.

Sincerely,
S.T.
(1967)

ANSWER:
Blessed be the grandmothers and grandfathers who brought with them to this country the spiritual values of generations deeply rooted in Jewish life. A great many of their American children and grandchildren did not show any interest in upholding and continuing this rich, spiritual heritage. That you do not now have the Jewish atmosphere you long for is in great part the fault of your parents because they did not carry on in the same tradition of your grandparents. Had they brought you up in the traditions of your grandfather, you would now have a circle of friends in which you could live as you desire.

The atmosphere, the life to which you are drawn, is usually not found in the suburbs. But if you were to come to

New York to study, you could find a circle of young people and the environment you long for.

JAPANESE PICTURE-BRIDES [3]

Like the Chinese pattern of immigration in the nineteenth century, very few Japanese women came to America in the early period of Japanese immigration during the late 1880s through the 1890s. Unlike the Chinese pattern, however, within a couple of decades many young Japanese males began to bring over wives. The turn of the century signaled the beginning of Japanese female immigration to America and it continued until the Japanese government curtailed it in 1920.

In 1900 out of the total Japanese population of 24,326 in America there were only 985 females—approximately 24 males for every female. During succeeding decades this ratio was significantly reduced with the arrival of additional females. In 1910 the number of females jumped to 9,087. By 1920 there were 22,193 out of the total population of 111,010.

The immigration of these women made the Japanese-American family unit possible and produced the second generation, marking the transition from a society of single male sojourners to permanent immigrants.

This remarkable demographic change stemmed from the so-called "picture-bride" practice. For the Japanese males in America, there were a number of ways to secure a spouse.

On the one hand, the problem was straightforward for those who had married prior to their emigration. Upon establishing themselves in this country, they simply summoned their wives to rejoin them.

But the problem was not as easily solved for the majority of Japanese males who were still single. If they had the opportunity, some married single Japanese women already here, but these marriage opportunities were rare.

[3] Article "Issei: The First Women," by Emma Gee. *Civil Rights Digest.* 5:48–53. Spring '74. This material is part of a collection gathered for an Asian-American studies program at the University of California, Berkeley.

Most single men resorted to one of two other ways to secure wives. Many returned to Japan to seek them—usually in their home villages—married while there, and then came back to America with their new brides. Though widely practiced, this method was not the most common, reserved as it was for those who had the economic means. For not only the return trip, but also the myriad of responsibilities of marriage in Japan entailed onerous expenses. Hence the majority of single Japanese males adopted the often misunderstood and maligned practice of selecting picture-brides.

Picture Brides

Picture-bride marriages grew out of the *omiai-kekkon* or arranged marriage. An agreed upon go-between or go-betweens carried out the negotiations between Japanese families throughout the selection process, and the initial customary meeting or *omiai* between prospective brides and bridegrooms often was preceded by an exchange of photographs, especially in cases in which the families were separated by long distance. Apart from the fact that the partners to a union neither met during the course of negotiations nor were both present at the wedding ceremony, the picture-bride marriage satisfied all the recognized social conventions regarding marriage in Japan.

Moreover, it became a legally recognized marriage as soon as the bride was entered in her new husband's family register. To apply for a passport to America, the bride was required by the Japanese government to present a certified copy of her husband's family register with her name entered in it for at least six months.

The Anti-Japanese Movement

The coming of the picture-bride added fuel to the anti-Japanese movement. One of the chief arguments against the Japanese was their "nonassimilability." To the rabid exclusionists, the picture-brides provided additional substantiation of this allegation, for they interpreted—and hence condemned—picture-bride marriages as an immoral social custom antithetical to American Christian ideals. That the

Japanese engaged in such a degrading practice was evidence of their nonassimilability.

In their condemnation of picture-brides, the exclusionists circulated exaggerated figures on Japanese fecundity, conjuring up the ominous specter of picture-brides breeding like rats and producing even more unassimilable Japanese. They also charged that picture-brides became laborers as soon as they set foot on American soil. Since the Japanese government had consented to curtail the emigration of laborers with the Gentlemen's Agreement of 1907-1908, the Japanese, according to the exclusionists, violated the spirit, if not the letter, of this agreement. Thus, immorality was linked to Japanese governmental treachery in the exclusionist's virulent attacks upon the picture-brides.

Because of these attacks and US government pressures, the Japanese government discontinued issuing passports to picture brides in 1920, which, along with the subsequent 1924 Immigration Act, left 42.5 percent of the adult Japanese males still single in America with no hopes of getting married—a cruel blow to a people who believed the saying "no matter what possessions a man may have, he is not a success unless he is married and has a family . . . to fail in this is to fail in life."

Pioneers

It is difficult for us to imagine the experience of the Issei (first generation) pioneer woman from the time of her marriage to her arrival and settlement in America. Excerpts from accounts written by some of them will provide some insight into their experience. How did she feel and think about her marriage and her future in America? One picture-bride comments on her husband: "I had but remote ties with him. Yet because of the talks between our close parents and my parents' approval and encouragement, I decided upon our picture-bride marriage."

The family in her specific case—indeed, in most marriages—had played the decisive role, and her decision was dependent upon it. But however the decision was arrived at, the prospects of coming to America must have been viewed with mixed emotions. On the one hand, there is the example of a wife whose husband had preceded her to America: "I was bubbling over with great expectations. My young heart, nineteen years and eight months old, burned not so much with the prospects of reuniting with my new husband, but with the thought of the New World."

Many women like her placed great store in America, and their glowing images of America accounted for their enthusiasm. This same person continues: "My husband who had returned to Japan to seek a wife wore a Western-style high-collar suit at our *omiai*. He told unusual stories about America which were like dreams to me. Being reared in the countryside, I listened intently with wide-opened eyes. Thus, I thought about how heavenly America was."

Attired in the latest Western suits, Japanese men who returned to Japan naturally told tales which, while not necessarily fictional, were probably embroidered to impress prospective brides. After all they were the "successful" individuals who had the economic means to return to Japan!

Other women received similar impressions from letters and photographs from their husbands-to-be in America who were equally anxious to secure wives. An element of vanity no doubt was intermingled, especially with a captive audience eager for news about foreign lands, and the tendency was toward the hyperbole.

Still there were husbands who were candid.

"My unknown husband had said," according to another picture-bride, " 'If you come with great expectations about living in an immigrant land, you will be disappointed.' I had received letters which said that if I intended to see things through without giving up, then I should come to America." And this particular woman, having this understanding clearly in mind, made the following resolution:

On the way from Kobe to Yokohama, gazing upon the rising majestic Mount Fuji in a cloudless sky aboard the ship, I made a resolve. For a woman who was going to a strange society and relying upon an unknown husband whom she had married through photographs, my heart had to be as beautiful as Mount Fuji. I resolved that the heart of a Japanese woman had to be sublime, like that soaring majestic figure eternally constant through wind and rain, heat, and cold. Thereafter, I never forgot that resolve on the ship, enabling me to overcome sadness and suffering.

Arriving in an Alien Land

The passage across the Pacific was a mixture of sadness at leaving Japan and apprehensions concerning the future. Having left families, relatives, and all that was familiar to them, now the women were actually en route to meet and live with their husbands in an alien land.

As soon as the women debarked, it was common for the husbands to whisk them to a clothing store. The Japanese were well aware that the Chinese had been excluded in 1882. Since the Chinese had not adopted Western-style clothing, the Japanese believed the Chinese had provided substance to the charge of being nonassimilable. To avoid the same accusation, Japanese husbands had their new brides fitted in a new set of Western clothing to replace the traditional Japanese kimono. A picture-bride described this event:

I was immediately outfitted [at] this Western clothing Store . . . At that time a suit of Western clothing cost from $25 to $28. Because I had to wear a tight corset around my chest, I could not bend forward. I had to have my husband tie my shoe laces.

There were some women who fainted because the corset was too tight. The stories of women being carried to the hotel rooms by their husbands who hurriedly untied the corset strings were not joking matters. In my case, I wore a large hat, a high-necked blouse, a long skirt, a buckled belt around my waist, high-laced shoes, and, of course, for the first time in my life, a brassiere and hip pads.

Once the initial encounter with America was over, their new life with their husbands began—and that was anything but easy. For not only did the brides have to adjust to an alien environment, they also had to establish a new household. On the lack of modern amenities a woman writes:

At the farm on Vashon Island [in Puget Sound, Washington] to which I went, I had to draw water by bucket from a well. . . .

I boiled water and put it into a tub. There was no electricity. I used oil lamps. No matter how backward Japan may have been, this was life in the hinterland. Still I toiled in sweat alongside my husband.

Most Issei women immediately began to work alongside their husbands. They could not afford a honeymoon. Besides doing the regular chores of cooking, washing, cleaning, and sewing, they labored long hours in fields or shops. A woman recounts her early agricultural work:

At the beginning I worked with my husband picking potatoes or onions and putting them in sacks. Working with rough-and-tumble men, I became weary to the bones; waking up in the mornings I could not bend over the wash basin.

Sunlight came out about 4:00 A.M. during the summer in the Yakima Valley [Washington]. I arose at 4:30. After cooking breakfast, I went out to the fields. There was no electric stove or gas like now. It took over one hour to cook, burning kindling wood.

As soon as I came home, I first put on the fire, took off my hat, and then I washed my hands. After cooking both breakfast and lunch, I went to the fields.

Work was neither less difficult nor shorter in the urban occupations. Take, for example, the case of a woman whose husband operated a laundry. After working the entire day, she records:

. . . I started at 5:00 P.M. to prepare supper for five to six persons, and then I began my evening work. The difficult ironing remained. Women's blouses in those days were made from silk or lace, with collars, and long sleeves and lots of frills.

I could only finish two in one hour, ironing them with great care. Hence, I worked usually until 12 to 1 A.M. But it was not just me—all women who worked in the laundry business probably did the same thing.

Starting a Family

Soon after these experiences with the harsh realities of life in America, Issei women began to bear children. In most rural areas where the Issei settled, doctors were not

readily available. Even if they were, either the white doctors refused treatment or the Japanese could not afford
them. No prenatal clinic existed. As a general rule, mid-
wives substituted for doctors during childbirth.

Problems of postnatal care and child-rearing naturally
followed successful childbirth. In households where the
women also performed crucial economic functions—especially in farming areas—a reasonable period of postnatal re-
cuperation was considered a luxury. An Issei woman com-
mented: "Twenty-one days of postnatal rest was common
even in Japan. Even busy housewives with household chores
to do took this twenty-one-day rest without doing anything.
I, however, could not rest for more than three days."

Most Issei women had to raise their children by themselves because of the sharp sexual division of labor within
the home. Even if they worked in the family economic unit,
they still had to carry the entire burden of housekeeping
and childrearing. As an Issei woman reveals:

My husband . . . did not think of helping in the house or with
the children. No matter how busy I may have been, he never
changed the baby's diapers. Though it may not be right to say
this ourselves, we Issei pioneer women from Japan worked solely
for our husbands. At mealtime, whenever there was not enough
food, we served a lot to our husbands and took very little for
ourselves.

Despite long, arduous hours of labor and the innumer-
able difficulties of childbirth and childrearing, the Issei
women persevered.

The "Quiet American"

From these brief excerpts, it is clear that these were truly
remarkable women. From their initial decision to come to
America, through the trans-Pacific voyage, and finally to
their adaptation to life in America, they had the physical
stamina and moral courage to persist and survive.

In spite of the primitive conditions, particularly in the
rural areas, they worked unremittingly with a minimum of
complaints. They never thought solely of their own welfare.
They thought more about giving than taking. They labored

beside their husbands and raised their children as best as they could within the framework of the beliefs and values they had been taught in late Meiji Japan [the period of the reign—1867-1912—of Emperor Mutsuhito].

Their lives were not sensational. Possessed of an extraordinary strength of character derived from quiet fortitude, the Issei women found life meaningful.

Many Sansei (third generation Japanese Americans) today are decrying the image of the "Quiet American" with some justification. Yet amid the clamor for social change, accompanied at times by loud political rhetoric, we should not disparage the quiet fortitude of these Issei women.

In America quietness and modesty tend to be equated with weakness. But with these Issei women quietness and modesty are sure signs of strength.

ASTORIA, THE LARGEST GREEK CITY OUTSIDE GREECE [4]

During the last two decades, when vibrant communities in many parts of New York City have declined, sometimes into virtual wastelands, a section of northwest Queens—Astoria—that was beginning to slump, has been turned around and is now booming. New homes have arisen, and old ones have been renovated. Empty stores have become prosperous businesses, and desolate buildings have become thriving factories.

This urban transformation has been provided by the Greek-Americans of Astoria, many of them immigrants, who have built in what was once a largely Italian area a community that is, in effect, the largest Greek city outside Greece.

This exotic city within a city is alive with Greek night-clubs, restaurants, tavernas, coffeehouses and exotic groceries. This is the area for Greek movies and shops offering

[4] From an article by Murray Schumach, staff writer. New York *Times*. p C 24. O. 7, '77. © 1977 by The New York Times Company. Reprinted by permission.

records and tapes of Greek music, Greek-style jewelry, ikons and ornaments and Greek magazines and newspapers.

In this world of between sixty thousand and seventy thousand Greek-Americans, a Greek Orthodox priest, the Rev. John Poulos—"Father John" to the people there—has far more influence than any politician. The children—sometimes despite a temporary language difficulty—are setting high educational standards. And almost everything in this community less than fifteen minutes by the RR line or the BMT subway from Times Square, is family-oriented—even the movies and nightclubs.

Greek is spoken and seen almost as often as English along spacious Ditmars Boulevard or under the elevated on Thirty-first Street or on the crowded sidewalks or stretches of Broadway. The trademark of the new neighborhood, which often leapfrogs blocks of Italian-American residents, is the red-brick, two-family house that almost always has three families in it.

History

The first Greeks are believed to have filtered in among the Germans, Irish and Italians of Astoria early in this century. There were certainly enough to fill a Trojan horse by 1927 because on October 28, 29 and 30 the "Hellenic Orthodox Community of Astoria" is celebrating its fiftieth anniversary.

Why the Greeks settled in Astoria is being worked up in a history for this month's golden anniversary. One theory is that the Greeks do not like apartment houses, and Astoria gave them homes with backyards.

The big shift of Greeks began in the 1950s. Immigration laws were eased in that decade and in the sixties, so that even those Greeks who had already gone to Australia or Canada because they could not get into the United States were now able to relocate in New York.

Equally important was the decline of such areas as the lower East Side, the midtown West Side and Washington Heights, simultaneously with the growing prosperity of

Greeks who had settled in them. Some of Astoria's Irish and Italian immigrants and their descendants were moving to the suburbs and were willing to sell their frame or shingle homes at reasonable prices. The Greek invasion was inexorable.

Church

The Greek life of Astoria revolves around the St. Demitrios parish: This is made up [of] two churches—St. Demitrios, at Thirty-first Street and Thirtieth Drive, and SS. Catherine and George, on Thirty-third Street, near Ditmars Boulevard. The Rev. John Poulos heads both.

These churches are much more than gathering places for religious services, baptisms and weddings. They find jobs, help in marital problems, find doctors for the ill, help newcomers locate an apartment and even furnish it.

And of particular importance is the parochial school from kindergarten through high school. Last year [1976-1977], 41 students from the elementary school took the exacting citywide test for admission to Stuyvesant High School, Brooklyn Technical High School and the Bronx High School of Science. It is an indicator of the school's quality that 39 passed.

The blue jackets and gray trousers or skirts of St. Demitrios students are badges of honor in Astoria. They are also guarantees that the children will get a great deal of homework.

Dancing

"Greeks work hard and they play hard," said Paul Calamaras, who with his brother, Tom, owns the Oyster Bay and the Crystal Palace, on Astoria's Broadway, near Thirty-first Street, the two major catering places and dance halls for the Greek community—Greeks come here from as far away as Canada and the West Coast. . . .

As Mr. Calamaras talked, music shrilled and pounded in the halls, and dancers formed circular, swirling chains. Occasionally, other guests showered the dancers with bills that would be swept up later for the musicians. The merriment was vigorous and contagious.

Mr. Calamaras strayed into another room where a wedding party was just becoming exuberant. He recognized a number of the guests.

Some of these people [he said] were at a party one night, I just couldn't get them out. They were supposed to stop about 3 o'clock. They didn't want to stop. They took off their shoes, and they kept dancing. At 5 o'clock I begged them to leave. I told them we had to get the room ready for a party at 10 o'clock that morning. They just laughed. I finally had to chase them out. The whole floor was covered with money for the musicians. The Greeks are good tippers.

The Crystal Palace is for dances. Its dance floors have already been booked into May on weekends. On Friday nights, the dances are usually for Greek college students.

But on Saturday nights they are usually more exciting. For these are by countrymen from the same districts of Greece. Astoria has many such clubs, where ordinarily, the men play cards and drink coffee. But for these dances they bring their own musicians to play their own dances. These are family affairs. However, visitors can watch the dancing by purchasing tickets at the door. . . .

Stores

In Astoria, the front of the store can be deceptive. On the sidewalk in front of 31-27 Ditmars Boulevard are stands of fruit. It looks like just another store for fruits and vegetables. But inside, the feta cheese is kept in a barrel in salt water. There are six kinds of olives. There is the *trusi*—a salad of carrots, green peppers, cauliflower, parsley, dill, vinegar and salt. There is the smoked herring called *renga*, the Greek salami known as *aeros*, the caviar spread known as *taramasalata* and jars of sour cherries, bitter orange, Greek bread and butter and olive oil. . . .

Or there is the Corfou Center, at 22-13 Thirty-first Street, which from the outside seems to specialize in newspapers and magazines flown in from Greece. Inside are sold tapes of Greek music, ikons, jewelry. . . .

Eating, Drinking, Talking

Where Greeks gather they usually eat, drink and talk. There is, for instance, the custom of the *zaharoplastion,* a difficult word for tables at which Greeks gather to sip strong coffee out of demitasses and to eat rich pastries. The day runs well past midnight at the Lefkos Pirgos, . . . where the family groups ignore calories to eat *bougatsa, milfae, petallouda* and, of course, *baklava.* . . .

Nothing is more Greek than the *taverna,* or *psistaria,* where an entire lamb turns on a spit, and beef, spinach pie, chicken and assorted Greek dishes are selected by customers, sometimes from the street, before they sit at tables.

At the Rumeli Taverna, . . . the food is wholesome and plentiful, and nothing on the menu is more than $4.50. Nearly everyone in the place seems Greek, happy and hungry, children as well as adults. Occasionally a man at one table buys a bottle of wine for those at another table. The wine is poured, but before it can be drunk, the recipients raise their glasses and call to their benefactor *"eis egia"*—to your health.

There are restaurants, such as the Vedeta, . . . which are more sedate. . . . And then there is the Stani, . . . which has entertainment beginning at 9 P.M. At both these places children come along with their parents. The Stani calls itself the "family nightclub."

For that matter, the Ditmars Theater, a movie house that shows only Greek films, calls itself "the family theater" and boasts all its movies are fit for children. . . .

An exception to the traditional pattern of Greek entertainment is the Bouat—a Greek variant of *boîte.* . . . Here the owner, Serafin Lazos, plays the guitar and sings modern Greek songs and occasionally one in Spanish as well. In this audience there are no children and very few patrons past the age of forty. These Greeks come to listen and applaud, sometimes at some special phrasing or fingering during a song. . . .

Perhaps the most extraordinary thing about the night life of Astoria is that people walk about the streets at two in the morning and seem to feel safe.

THE SIGNIFICANCE OF THE MEXICAN-AMERICAN PEOPLE [5]

Most [Mexican-Americans] live in the states of California, Arizona, New Mexico, Texas, and Colorado, but a large number have made homes in the greater Chicago area and in other industrial centers. In many sections of the Southwest, particularly along the border from San Diego, California, to Brownsville, Texas, Mexican-Americans are the majority population, and their language and culture serve to provide the entire region with much of its charm and distinctiveness.

Modern-day Mexican-Americans play a vital role in the industrial, agricultural, artistic, intellectual, and political life of the Southwest but the significance of this group cannot be measured solely in terms of present-day accomplishments. It is certain that the Southwest as we know it would not exist without the Mexican-Spanish heritage. That which sets New Mexico off from Oklahoma and California off from Oregon is in large measure the result of the activities of the ancestors of our fellow citizens of Mexican descent. Our way of life has been and is being immeasurably enriched by their presence north of the present-day international boundary. . . .

In what is now the United States Mexicans were active in the development of new mining regions (gold was discovered in California in 1842, for example), opening up new routes for travelers (as from Santa Fe to Los Angeles via Las Vegas, Nevada), founding schools (some twenty-two teachers were brought to California in the 1830s and a seminary was

[5] From article by Dr. Jack D. Forbes, research director, Far West Laboratory; member, national advisory council, Multi-Culture Institute; educator and author specializing in ethnohistory and applied anthropology. In *The Chicanos in America, 1540–1974*, edited by R. A. Garcia. Oceana. '77. p 25–34. The article appeared originally in *Mexican-Americans: A Handbook for Educators*, a report prepared for the United States Department of Health, Education, and Welfare in 1970.

established at Santa Ynez), establishing new towns (Sonoma, California, is an example), and setting up printing presses (as in California in 1835). . . .

Mexican Miners and Colonists in the North

Commencing in the 1830s Mexican settlers began moving north once again. Some two hundred craftsmen, artisans, and skilled laborers sailed to California in that decade, and soon overland immigrants from Sonora were joining them. Thereafter a steady stream of Sonorans reached California, only to be turned into a flood by the discovery of gold in the Sierra Nevada foothills in 1848. The Sonorans were often experienced miners and their techniques dominated the California Gold Rush until steam-powered machinery took over at a later date. Chihuahuans and other Mexicans also "rushed" to California by sea and by land and they too exercised an impact upon mining as well as upon commerce.

The United States–Mexican War of 1846-1848 did not immediately alter the character of the Southwest greatly, except in eastern Texas and northern California. The Gold Rush changed the language of central California after 1852 (when Mexican miners were largely expelled from the Sierra Nevada mines), but Mexicans continued to dominate the life of the region from San Luis Obispo, California, to San Antonio, Texas. Southern California, for example, remained a Spanish-speaking region until the 1870s with Spanish-language and bilingual public schools, Spanish-language newspapers, and Spanish-speaking judges, elected officials, and community leaders. The first Constitution of the State of California, created in part by persons of Mexican background, established California as a bilingual state and it remained as such until 1878. Similar conditions prevailed in other southwestern regions.

Anglo-Americans Become Dominant

Gradually, however, Anglo-Americans from the East who were unsympathetic toward Mexican culture came to dominate the Southwest. Having no roots in the native soil and being unwilling to become assimilated to the region, these newcomers gradually transformed the schools into English-language institutions where no Spanish was taught, constructed buildings with an "eastern" character, pushed Mexican leaders into the background, and generally caused the Mexican-American, as he has come to be termed, to become a forgotten citizen.

By the 1890s on the other hand, tourists and writers began to rediscover the "Spanish" heritage and "landmark" clubs commenced the process of restoring the decaying missions of the Southwest. A "Spanish" cultural revival was thus initiated, and soon it began to influence architectural styles as well as the kind of pageantry which has typified much of the Southwest ever since. Unfortunately, the Mexican-Indian aspect of the region's heritage was at first overlooked and the Mexican-American people benefited but little from the emphasis upon things Spanish.

Twentieth Century Mexican "Pioneers"

In the early 1900s a new group of Mexican immigrants began to enter the United States, attracted by job offers from agricultural developers who wished to open up virgin lands in southern California, Colorado, Arizona, and south Texas. During World War I and the 1920s this movement became a flood, a flood which largely overwhelmed the older group of Mexican-Americans (except in northern New Mexico and southern Colorado) and became ancestral to much of the contemporary Spanish-speaking population in the Southwest.

These hundreds of thousands of new Mexican-Americans had to overcome many obstacles as they attempted to improve their life patterns. Anglo-Americans were prejudiced against people who were largely of Native American, brown-skinned origin, who were poor, who of necessity lived in substandard or self-constructed homes, who could not speak English, and who were not familiar with the workings of a highly competitive and acquisitive society. Gradually, and in spite of the trauma of the Great Depression (when all sorts of pressures were used to deport Mexican-Americans to Mexico), *los de la raza* [those of the race], as Mexicans in the United States frequently refer to themselves, climbed the economic ladder and established stable, secure communities in the Southwest.

Development of the Mexican-American Community

The Mexican-American community was not simply a passive force during this long period of transition. Everywhere mutual benefit societies, patriotic Mexicanist organizations, newspapers, social clubs, small stores and restaurants were founded, and artisans began to supply Anglo-American homes with pottery and other art objects (the first gift I ever gave to my mother was a pottery bowl made by a Mexican-American craftsman who fashioned ceramics in a shop behind his home on our street in El Monte, California).

Mexican-American mutual benefit organizations soon commenced the task of helping to upgrade the status of agricultural and industrial workers by seeking better wages and conditions of employment. During the 1920s and 1930s Mexican-American labor organizers, with little formal education and less money, traveled from region to region, helping in the unionization process. Ever since, labor leaders have played an important role in Mexican-American affairs and Spanish-speaking union officers are a significant element in the structure of organized labor in the Southwest. Current efforts directed toward the unionization of agricultural workers and obtaining a minimum wage for agricultural laborers, from California to south Texas, are being led by organizers of Mexican ancestry.

During the past twenty years the cultural and political life of Mexican-Americans has advanced remarkably. Today, fine Spanish-language newspapers blanket the Southwest and Far West, some of which are daily periodicals with the latest dispatches from Europe and Mexico. Magazines, including bilingual ones, issue forth with slick paper and exciting photographs. Spanish-language radio and television stations reach much of the Southwest, and theatrical-musical productions of a folk or modern nature are frequently staged for the benefit of both *los de la raza* and Anglos.

Mexican-American civic, business and political leaders are now prominent in many regions, and they include within their ranks members of Congress, mayors, and all types of professional people. The image of the Mexican heritage has vastly improved due not only to the activities of individual Mexican-Americans, but also due to the cultural renaissance occurring in Mexico itself concurrent with the incredible richness of the Mexican past revealed by contemporary archeological discoveries. Anglo-Americans have ceased emphasizing the Spanish legacy at the expense of the Mexican, and a more healthy climate of mutual understanding has evolved.

Educational Progress

Educationally, Mexican-American progress has been striking in individual cases but has been slow overall. Generally speaking, whenever Anglo-Americans gained control over a particular state or region in the Southwest they chose to import the kinds of public schools developed in the Middle West or East. Hispano-Mexican and bilingual schools were replaced by English-language, Anglo-oriented schools from which Mexican-American children were sometimes excluded. After the turn of the century greater numbers of Spanish-speaking youth began to attend schools, but the latter were either irrelevant to the background, language, and interests of the pupils (as in New Mexico) or were segregated, marginal elementary schools (as in much of California and Texas). Normally, secondary-level education was not available to Mexican-American pupils except in an alien Anglo-dominated school (and even that opportunity was often not present in many rural counties in Texas and elsewhere).

During the post–World War II period segregated schools for Mexican-Americans largely disappeared, except where residential segregation operated to preserve the ethnic school. Greater numbers of Mexican-Americans entered high school and enrollment in college also increased, although slowly. Nevertheless, dropout rates remain high, even today; and it is also true that the typical school serving

Mexican-Americans makes little, if any, concession to the Mexican heritage, the Spanish language, or to the desires of the Mexican-American community.

A Six-Thousand-Year-Old Heritage

In summary, the Mexican heritage of the United States is very great indeed. For at least six thousand years Mexico has been a center for the dissemination of cultural influences in all directions, and this process continues today. Although the modern United States has outstripped Mexico in technological innovation, the Mexican people's marked ability in the visual arts, music, architecture, and political affairs makes them a constant contributor to the heritage of all of North America. The Mexican-American people of the United States serve as a bridge for the diffusion northward of valuable Mexican traits, serve as a reservoir for the preservation of the ancient Hispano-Mexican heritage of the Southwest, and participate directly in the daily life of the modern culture of the United States.

The Mexican-American Way of Life

The United States' . . . citizens of Mexican origin do not form a homogeneous group with identical values, customs, and aspirations. One can divide the Mexican-American community along class (economic) lines, from the affluent rancher, businessman, or public official to the migrant farm worker or isolated self-sufficient farmer in the mountains of New Mexico. One can also divide the Mexican-American community on the basis of the degree to which the individual has become Anglicized and integrated into the larger society. One can further classify Mexican-Americans according to the degree of Caucasian ancestry which they possess, or according to whether or not they object to being called "Mexicans" and prefer to be called "Spanish-American." But whichever type of classification system one uses, it is clear that there is no single way of life possessed by our Mexican-American people.

Nonetheless, it is possible for purposes of generalization to ignore those individuals who are nontypical and to concentrate upon the large majority of Mexican-Americans who have many things in common.

First, the Mexican-American community is basically proud of being of Mexican background and sees much of value in the Mexican heritage. By means of folk-level educational agencies, such as benevolent societies, patriotic organizations, and the extended family, many Mexican traits are kept alive, either as functioning parts of the individual's personal life or at least as items with which he feels some degree of familiarity. Mexican arts and crafts, music, dances, cooking, family structure, concepts of the community, the Spanish language, and other characteristics, are maintained in this manner. Spanish-language radio and television stations, newspapers, and magazines, and Mexican-American political organizations, help to carry on this process as well as to bring in new cultural influences from Mexico. In short, the Mexican-American community possesses many internal agencies which serve to maintain a sense of belonging to *la raza* and which also serve to carry forward worthy aspects of the Mexican heritage.

In many rural areas of the Southwest, as well as in some wholly Mexican urban districts, most adults can be described as belonging primarily to the culture of northern Mexico. The Spanish language is universally favored over English and the bilateral extended family provides a satisfying and strong social background for the individual. In other urban districts, as well as in suburban regions and on the fringes of Mexican neighborhoods in rural areas, one finds numerous Mexican-Americans who are completely bilingual, or who in some cases favor English over Spanish. These people have not become "Anglos," but their Mexican cultural heritage has become blended with Anglo-American traits.

Unfortunately, many younger Mexican-Americans, educated in Anglo-oriented schools, have not been able to relate in a positive manner toward either the north Mexican or Mexican-Anglo mixed cultures, primarily because their parents have been unable to effectively transmit the Spanish language and Mexican heritage to them. At the same time the public schools have either attacked or completely ignored their heritage and have attempted to substitute an often watered-down Anglo heritage. The youth subjected to this pressure have not ordinarily become Anglos, though, because of a feeling of being rejected by the dominant society (because of frequently experienced prejudice and discrimination) and by the schools (because the curriculum is so totally negative as regards their own personal and cultural background). These young people have frequently developed a mixed Anglo-Mexican subculture of their own, based upon a dialect of Spanish heavily modified by an ingenious incorporation of English words and new expressions and upon a "gang" style of social organization.

Another important factor which retards the complete absorption of partially Anglicized Mexican-Americans into the larger society is the fact that more than 95 percent of Mexicans are part-Indian, 40 percent are full-blood Indians, and most of the mixed-bloods have more Indian than non-Indian ancestry. Mexican-Americans are, therefore, a racial as well as a cultural minority and the racial differences which set them apart from Anglos cannot be made to "disappear" by any "Americanization" process carried on in the schools.

The larger Mexican-American community is in a process of rapid cultural transition, wherein most individuals are acquiring a mixed Anglo-Mexican culture, while smaller numbers are marrying into or otherwise being absorbed into the dominant Anglo society. An unfortunate aspect of this process is that extremely valuable Mexican traits such as the strong extended family, the tendency toward mutual aid, the Spanish language, artistic and musical traditions, folk dances, fine cooking, and such personality characteristics as placing more emphasis upon warm interpersonal relationships than upon wealth acquisition tend to be replaced by what many critics might suggest are the lowest common denominator of materialistic, acquisitive, conformist traits typical of some elements within the Anglo-American population. That this is occurring is largely a result of the fact that many Mexican-American graduates of the public schools feel ambivalent about their own self-identity and about cultural values. They have been deprived of a chance to learn about the best of the Mexican heritage and at the same time, have been, in effect, told to become Anglicized. They tend, therefore, to drift into the dominant society without being able to make sound value-judgements based upon cross-cultural sophistication.

On the other hand, the Mexican-American community considered in its entirety is a vital, functioning societal unit with considerable ability to determine its own future course of development. It may well succeed in developing a reasonably stable bicultural and bilingual tradition which will provide a healthy atmosphere for future generations and which may prove attractive to many Anglos. In any case it is clear that the proximity of Mexico will insure a continual flow of Mexican cultural influences across the border and the Mexican-American community, as a bicultural population, will not soon disappear.

ETHNIC SUCCESSION IN AMERICA [6]

It is evident from even a cursory study of many of our institutions that they are heavily influenced and sometimes dominated by various racial, religious and ethnic groups. Large-scale power and decision-making areas have traditionally been in older stock, Protestant hands. Throughout America's history, people of English, Scottish, Welsh, Dutch and German backgrounds have occupied top positions in government, science, education and the military. The pre-eminence of these groups in these areas is due, in part, to the fact that they had overwhelmingly represented the majority in this country from the colonial period until this century when the great influx of immigrants changed the balance.

America's financial and industrial executive suites are

[6] From pamphlet entitled *Moving Up*, by Daniel Elazar and Murray Friedman. Institute on Pluralism and Group Identity. 165 E. 56th St. New York, NY 10022. '76. p 6–13. Copyright © 1976 by the Institute on Pluralism and Group Identity of the American Jewish Committee. All rights reserved. Reprinted by permission. Daniel Elazar is an author, journalist, and professor of political science, Temple University; Murray Friedman is an educator, lecturer, and writer.

still largely controlled by British-American and north European groups. Research shows that white Protestant leadership in key economic areas actually increased during the years 1900 to 1950. This same trend has been reflected in our political life as well. With only one exception, every United States President has come from a Protestant background and has usually been affiliated with an Episcopalian, Unitarian or Presbyterian church.

Patterns

America's racial, religious and ethnic groups have gravitated to or been pressed into certain fields of work which, in and of themselves, may have no special ethnic relatedness. In large measure, this is a result of the migration process. "As ethnic representatives invested their labor and talents in specific areas of activity," Dennis Clark writes, "they drew with them in a natural fashion family members, associates and clients. Eventually they became identified with certain enterprises, reinforcing this identification with an ethnic prominence that served to augment their business and community status."

Jews, for example, have traditionally been active in such areas as family-style businesses, sales and small manufacturing and lower and middle rungs of the civil service. The Irish have been drawn to local politics and government, particularly to the civil service. They are also heavily involved in the construction industry. Protestant and Catholic Germans, according to [sociologist] Andrew Greeley, tend to overchoose engineering careers. Slavic groups have constituted a significant portion of the work force in our coal mines and steel mills. These patterns are visible even within less orthodox forms of economic venture. Mark Haller's study of organized crime in Chicago shows that different ethnic groups have specialized in gambling, loan sharking, fencing, bootlegging and other forms of illegitimate enterprise. The development of ethnic divisions of labor is frequently interpreted to demonstrate that certain groups are naturally drawn to or innately suited for certain fields of work. While there may be certain affinities involved, it is dangerous to make blanket judgments in such matters.

The pattern of ethnic division of labor is found throughout the world among ethnic groups who share a common habitat, neighborhood or social experience. The phenomenon of guest labor—foreigners recruited for European industry—is now inflaming group tensions on the Continent. Between World Wars I and II, Malayans worked in rice plantations and Indians in rubber plantations in Malaysia, while the work force in the mines was primarily Chinese. Most Eurasians worked as clerks, while the Chinese operated the retail trade. In the Ituri forest in the Congo basin, Pygmies and their taller hosts live next to each other with the former providing honey and meat and the latter plantains.

Origins of Patterns

Although the relationship of America's ethnic groups to certain occupations has not been systematically investigated, we can reasonably speculate about the origin and history of these patterns. As the first arrivals—and, subsequently the best-positioned group—British-Americans and ethnically similar groups came to occupy socially, economically and politically advantaged or prestigious positions although, of course, many remained at the lower rungs of the social and economic ladder. These groups shared a common sense of individualism and enterprise frequently identified as the "Protestant ethic" which has heavily influenced social and cultural patterns.

Many Irish immigrants, predominantly poor and unskilled, began life here as manual workers. For those with energy and ambition, it was a natural progression from manning a shovel and wheelbarrow to becoming small, and later, large contractors. Religious discrimination and a separate religious tradition led the Irish to build a network of churches, schools and welfare institutions which provided a continuing source of construction opportunities.

Their knowledge of English and their quick grasp of American-style politics also opened up a variety of positions in city government and the civil service in general.

Even though many were poor, Jews came to America with a tradition that valued education. Many also arrived with a highly developed mercantile tradition but discrimination denied them entry into many areas of economic life. Jews gravitated to occupations where they could advance on the basis of individual merit. Jewish peddlers went into small retail businesses, a few of which evolved into enormous department stores. . . . They entered into government service and public school positions, independent businesses and professional fields of law and medicine and, most recently, into college and university teaching. Circumstances pushed the more enterprising into newer or sometimes more precarious economic areas such as the garment industry, entertainment, electronics and real estate.

Similarly, Italians found the road from rags to riches difficult. Generally unskilled and from peasant backgrounds, they arrived without the social supports of church, politics, city contacts and contracts. Initially, many worked as ditch diggers, section hands on railroads, shoemakers, barbers and garment workers. Today, many Italians are very much involved in the fields of construction, public service and the mass media as well as the professions.

We have attempted to suggest the historical relationship of ethnicity to certain occupations. The major factors in this interrelationship are a group's social, historical and cultural experiences. To some degree, the effects of racial or ethnic exclusion were mitigated by the American creed of equal opportunity. It is important to recognize that class position in our society is not the simple Horatio Alger process Americans celebrate; it has varied along racial, religious and ethnic lines.

The Process of Upward Mobility

By and large, while the first generation of immigrants has been locked into less remunerative and less prestigious occupations, succeeding generations have achieved positions of higher status. With few exceptions, blacks and other nonwhite minorities have not shared in this potential for upward mobility. As Peter M. Blau and Otis Dudley Duncan said . . . "Negroes are handicapped at every step in their attempts to achieve success, and these cumulative disadvantages are what produced the great inequalities of opportunities under which the Negro American suffers." (*The American Occupation Structure*, 1967)

It is apparent that groups begin to move up, share power with other groups and sometimes replace each other in different areas of American life. This process has not yet been clearly examined or understood. In *The Newcomers,* Oscar Handlin [historian, educator] traces the residential movement of older Dutch, English, Welsh, German and French families in the late 1800s from New York's lower East Side to their entrenchment in the favored sections of Greenwich Village and the east side of Manhattan as a result of the impact of the "new immigration" from southern and eastern Europe.

Now we see the southern and eastern Europeans are being replaced by the movement of blacks and Puerto Ricans into these neighborhoods. In this exchange, the displaced groups often take with them the intangible as well as the tangible things that give a community its unique flavor, such as ethnic restaurants, stores, special gathering places and even the name and prestige of a particular school. In turn, the newer groups bring their own distinctive characteristics and institutions with them into the area.

Just as neighborhoods have been changed, so too has the ethnic composition of industry and business been altered as newcomers began to penetrate the economic structures. In the industrially expansive period of the late nineteenth and early twentieth centuries, earlier groups that were displaced frequently moved up socially and economically, so that the strains of ethnic succession were eased somewhat. Southern and eastern European immigrants took over many of the lower status jobs throughout the economy. Many of the older immigrant employees from Great Britain and northern Europe moved up to become their supervisors and foremen.

In the late 1800s, a few German Jewish merchants who started as peddlers began the saga of turning small retail establishments into major department stores. "For the most part," Rudolf Glanz writes, "the Jews merely inherited the mantle of Yankees who had 'gone up' in the world." (*Studies in Judaica Americana,* 1970). This pattern, however, varied in different parts of the country. The New York garment industry, which initially had a heavy Jewish and Italian work force, is now largely composed of Puerto Ricans and blacks, with a new influx of Chinese women.

The sports and entertainment fields have traditionally provided attractive possibilities for upward mobility to "ethnic outs" who had few contacts or marketable skills in the established business world. At one time, the Irish and Jews played major roles in these areas. They were followed by Italians and, most recently, by blacks, Puerto Ricans and Cubans.

The political world provides the most dramatic and visible form of ethnic succession. Control of our cities' political machinery passed successively from older stock, Protestant hands to the Irish and then to Jews, Italians and other ethnic groups. Samuel Lubell provides a classic picture of the transfer of political power to new groups represented by the candidacy of Al Smith in 1928 and the election of Franklin D. Roosevelt four years later (*The Future of American Politics,* 1956). Since the civil rights movement and race revolts of the 1960s, the growth of black political power has been illustrated by the election of black mayors in Cleveland, Gary, Newark, Detroit, Los Angeles and Atlanta.

Cultural leadership has followed a similar path of ethnic succession. In the field of literature, Jewish, black and Catholic writers in the 1930s and 1940s began the long climb which made them the successors of such writers as Sinclair Lewis, Ernest Hemingway and William Faulkner. Norman Podhoretz credits Saul Bellow as breaking down the old-stock literary tradition that held other regional and ethnic traditions in "colonial subjugation" and opening up the possibility of "literary pluralism."

What Bellow the writer is saying is this:

> I am an American novelist, born into a Yiddish-speaking household and also educated to use fancy English with the best of them, and the way I speak as a result of these two facts, the way I really speak when I am being myself . . . is a fully legitimate literary language. . . . (*Making It,* 1968)

The passing on of power is not necessarily a result of older established groups being pushed out, although there are often bitter struggles. Many of the older stock, elite Protestant leadership were lured to the greater monetary reward of newly burgeoning industry in the nineteenth century; others simply transferred their political interests to another sphere. . . .

The Significance of Cultural Variation

The central questions to be examined are how do various ethnic groups move up in our social system and what role does ethnicity play in this process. Many Italians and Poles have not achieved the educational, occupational and financial success of their Catholic Irish, German and Jewish predecessors. It seems clear that this in no way relates to the innate intelligence of various groups—Arthur Jensen [educator, proponent of a theory of black genetic inferiority] notwithstanding—but rather has much to do with their social and cultural environments.

Ivan Light (in *Ethnic Enterprise in America,* 1972) compares the success the Chinese and Japanese have had in creating a business class in America to the difficulties that blacks have experienced, despite the similar patterns of discrimination and disadvantage that each group encountered. He traces this to the ethnic groups' social systems and the supports they received from these systems. All three groups arrived with informal rotating credit systems that provided a source of financial assistance unavailable to them in banks. But slavery, and the system of peonage that followed, prevented blacks from adapting this system of rotating credit to their new environment.

Susan S. Stodolsky and Gerald Lesser have demonstrated that certain educational skills or propensities remain constant for various ethnic groups regardless of whether members are middle or lower class. (They point out that relative to the general population Jews score higher in verbal ability than they do in space conceptualization. For Chinese children, this is exactly reversed.) Manuel Ramirez III has found cultural differences in motivation: Anglo children are conditioned to be competitive and individually socially mobile; Chicano children value group cooperation, which is more consistent with their culture's strong kinship ties. Aesthetic expression is a dominant characteristic of Japanese culture, while verbal expression is characteristic of Jewish and Italian culture. How children learn may have a much greater cultural variation than we previously believed. Educators who lack "cultural competence" may be doing a disservice to their students.

It is clear that ethnic background affects values, communication and self-identification patterns and community structures, which in turn are related to occupational motivation and choices. At this point, our information is limited and far from synthesized, but is beginning to prove that ethnicity, even among second and third generation Americans, counts—often a great deal.

"Making It" in America

The phenomenon of group success is partly related to the similarity between the value systems, lifestyles and even physical appearance of the newer groups and those of the older, established ethnic groups. Even so, our early history is filled with episodes of conflict between various Protestant groups. Many earlier disputes have been resolved, but remnants of these struggles still exist and are reflected denominationally. While the earlier groups have largely merged structurally and culturally, the phenomenon of "Protestant particularism" is still alive.

The earlier groups' attitudes to later immigrants were conditioned on whether the latter were seen as potential competitors in the economic realm or as bearers of alternative values that challenged an established way of life. The large-scale exclusion of Jews from executive suites of top corporations, while not as total as a few years ago, is a major example of the still lingering suspicion of differing business styles and social values. For newer groups which have sharply different cultural backgrounds and have experienced significant discrimination and disadvantage, the process of ethnic succession often involves fierce competition between "ethnic outs" and "ethnic ins."

In these collisions, the "ethnic outs" draw upon group support systems as well as any assistance the broader society may provide such as recent antidiscrimination laws and affirmative action programs. As [sociologist] Lewis Coser notes, ethnic conflicts provide an important safety valve for releasing resentments and also help to restructure our social and economic relationships. The alternative to refusing to let the "outs" in is seen in many parts of the world today where ethnic conflict flares into violence.

America's system of ethnic succession is based on certain "rules of the game" that we have, by and large, accepted to maintain community peace and progress. The system works in the following way. Occupational specialization in our society has led to the domination of certain fields by one or a few ethnic groups. Unless attracted by opportunities elsewhere, these "ethnic ins" seek to maintain and augment their favorable position. Newer groups attempting to enter these fields must accept subordinate roles. Newer groups become dissatisfied with their subsidiary place and eventually attempt to challenge the status quo. At this point a struggle commences. The capacity of the "outs" to change the situation depends on the complex interaction of their potential social and political power, their willingness to use unorthodox tactics to make their claims on the system, the extent of opposition to them, and their ability to evoke sympathy for the past injustices they have suffered. [See "The Ethnic Miracle" in Section V, below.]

This process was historically seen in the heavy rioting of Protestant laborers in Philadelphia in 1844 when Bishop Kendrick demanded the elimination of the King James

(Protestant) Bible and the substitution of the Douay Bible for Catholic public school children. Upper class Protestant leaders such as George Templeton Strong, an old-line New Yorker, at first greeted the violence as strengthening the hands of the "natives." As the disorders grew, Strong confided his growing fears to his diary. On July 8 he recorded, "Civil War raging in Philadelphia . . . I shan't be caught voting for a 'native' ticket again in a hurry." As a result, the pressures of Bishop Kendrick, Archbishop Hughes in New York and other Catholic leaders led to the modification of the Protestant domination of the public schools and the eventual secularization of schools.

WHY CAN'T THEY BE LIKE US? [7]

When the social historians of, let us say, the twenty-third or twenty-fourth century look back on the era that we now presume to describe as the modern world, they will find two or three social phenomena of extraordinary interest. One, certainly, is the demographic revolution—the astonishing increase in the population level of the world that has occurred in the past century and a half. The second will be the westernization and industrialization of the non-Western world. And the third, unless I miss my guess, will be the formation of a new nation on the North American continent made up of wildly different nationality groups. The historians of the future will find it hard to believe it could have happened that English, Scotch, and Welsh, Irish, Germans, Italians, and Poles, Africans, Indians, both Eastern and Western, Frenchmen, Spaniards, Finns, Swedes, Lebanese, Danes, Armenians, Croatians, Slovenians, Greeks, and Luxembourgers, Chinese, Japanese, Filipinos and Puerto Ricans would come together to form a nation that not only would survive, but, all things considered, survive reasonably well. I further suspect that the historians of the future will be astonished that American sociologists, the product of this gathering in of the nations, could stand in the midst of such

[7] From Introduction to a pamphlet by Andrew M. Greeley, sociologist, author, program director, National Opinion Research Center. *Why Can't They Be Like Us*. Institute of Human Relations Press. '69. p 4–13. Reprinted with permission of Institute of Human Relations Press. All rights reserved.

an astonishing social phenomenon and take it so much for granted that they would not bother to study it.

They will find it especially astonishing in light of the fact that ethnic differences, even in the second half of the twentieth century, proved far more important than differences in philosophy or economic system. Men who would not die for a premise or a dogma or a division of labor would more or less cheerfully die for a difference rooted in ethnic origins. Chinese and Malay fight each other in Southeast Asia; Ibo and Hausa in Nigeria; Greek and Turk on Cyprus; Czech and Slovak in Czechoslovakia; Arab and Jew in the Middle East; black (at least so-called) fights white (at least relatively) in the United States; and the French and the English, running out of colonial peoples with which to contend, now renew the feud that the Hundred Years' War never did settle. Finally, along the lines of the Shamrock curtain, another feud simmers, and [Irish man of letters] Frank O'Connor's immortal words, spoken from the secure position of his own agnosticism, are as true as ever: "The north of Ireland contains the best Protestants in the world and the south of Ireland the best Catholics, and there is nary a single Christian in the whole lot."

Immigration, Acculturation, Assimilation

Fashions in thinking, both popular and scholarly, about ethnic groups have changed. It was first assumed that the cultural forces of American society, particularly as applied in the public school system, would rather shortly level the differences among American immigrant groups and that most of the immigrants would, in effect, become good white Anglo-Saxon Protestants, speaking what Professor Peter Rossi [former director, National Opinion Research Center; currently chairman, sociology department, Johns Hopkins University] once labeled "radio-standard English." Even though the naive "melting pot" notion has long since lost its scholarly respectability, it is still, one suspects, a latent but powerful influence in American society. As members of older immigrant groups say of members of younger immigrant groups, "Why don't they act like us?"

More recently, the idea of "cultural pluralism" emerged, which saw the United States not only as a nation of immigrants, but as a nation of immigrant groups; the immigrants, it was explained, would become American and thoroughly American, but at the same time retain much that was distinctive and creative about their own cultural heritage, perhaps even including their own language. A good deal of romantic prose has been written about how one nation is formed out of many, and about how Poles, Armenians, Italians, Jews, Irish, Hungarians and any other ethnic group one cares to mention can retain their own traditions and still be thoroughly and completely American.

Somewhere between the melting pot and cultural pluralism is the notion of the "multiple melting pot," first advanced by Ruby Joe Reeves Kennedy and made popular by Will Herberg [*Protestant—Catholic—Jew*. Doubleday. 1955]. In this view the old immigrant groups were collapsing, but three superethnic groups based on religion were replacing them. One would, therefore, no longer think of oneself as German or Swedish or Irish or Rumanian, but rather as Protestant, Catholic, or Jew.

A more sophisticated social science approach has been developed recently under the influence of S. N. Eisenstadt [*Essays on Comparative Social Change*. Wiley, 1965] and Milton Gordon [*Assimilation in American Life*. Oxford University Press, 1964], who hypothesize two kinds of assimilation: cultural assimilation or acculturation, which involves the process of the immigrant group learning the manners and the style of a new society, and structural assimilation (or simply assimilation) in which the members of the immigrant group relate to members of other groups, particularly on the intimate levels of friendship and family formation, without any regard to ethnic differences. Eisenstadt and Gordon suggest that acculturation is taking place among immigrant groups, but not assimilation. Irish, Polish, Jews, blacks, Armenians, Rumanians, Greeks, and so on, dress in the same kind of clothes, read the same magazines, watch the same television shows, perform the same kinds of jobs, share the same kinds of political and social values, but still, to a very considerable extent, seek their intimate friends and their marriage partners from within their own ethnic group. According to this theory, acculturation can go on at a relatively rapid rate, and even create a certain pressure for assimilation without making assimilation anywhere near complete, and therefore ethnic groups continue to survive and probably will do so for the foreseeable future. This assimilation-acculturation view seems to combine the best perspective of both the melting-pot and the cultural-pluralism approaches, but this does not necessarily mean that it is the best possible explanation for what's going on.

Another suggestion is found, however implicitly, in the excellent books written by Daniel Patrick Moynihan and Nathan Glazer [*Beyond the Melting Pot*. Harvard and MIT University Press, 1963] and Herbert Gans [*Urban Villagers*. Free Press, 1962]. These writers tend to view ethnic groups as essentially interest groups, which came into being because of common origin and cultural background and continue in existence as the most appropriate units through which their members can seek greater political, social and economic power for themselves. Their assumption is that cultural differences among ethnic groups are declining rapidly, if they have not already been eliminated, and that it is the common interest in political and socioeconomic power which keeps the groups together.

There is nowhere near enough empirical data to make any confident assertions about the validity of the various approaches described above. Nevertheless, my colleague Peter Rossi and I are inclined to view the last two described with some reservation. We do not want to deny that the ethnic communities are very powerful interest groups; nor that acculturation seems to be going on at a faster rate than assimilation. But we are still forced to wonder why common national origin would be the basis for organizing and sustaining an interest group, and we would also wonder whether even acculturation has gone on quite as rapidly as some observers might think. . . .

In other words, we are not ready to assume that vast

cultural differences do not persist. Our suspicion—and given the present state of the data, it is little more than suspicion —is that the core of these differences has to do with different expectations about close relatives; that is, in one ethnic group the expectations of how a husband or a wife, a father or a mother, a brother or a sister, a cousin, an aunt, or an uncle should behave are likely to be quite different than in another ethnic group. There is enough legend about Jewish mothers and Irish mothers for us to be able to realize that the expectations of these two ethnic groups, while in some sense quite similar, are also very, very different. But if we throw into the discussion the somewhat less known expectations of how a Missouri Synod German Lutheran mother ought to behave, we become quite conscious of how complex the question of the survival of ethnic differences really is.

The question is made even more complex by the fact that the various immigrant groups came here at different times, both in the development of the society they left behind and in the development of American society.

European Origins and American Experience

As [sociologist] Nathan Glazer has pointed out, the Germans came from a society that was a nation long before it had become a state, and many of the German immigrants saw no reason why they could not create a German nation in the midst of the American continent (and as part of the American Republic). The Irish were not so inclined to create an Irish nation, although on one occasion they did attempt to invade Canada to take it away from England. But both these groups came quite conscious of their nationality, and quite capable of setting up ethnic enclaves, whether in rural Iowa or urban Boston (the Germans chose the country far more than did the Irish), that were based on the concept of nationality.

The second type of immigrant group, according to Glazer, was the Scandinavians who indeed came from states, but states that were not yet nations; for the Scandinavian peasants saw themselves less as members of nations than citizens of villages or members of a religious community. The Norwegians and the Swedes came to think of themselves as Norwegians and Swedes only when they banded together here to form communities of their fellows, particularly in the rural areas where the Scandinavians tended to settle. Glazer observed that it was easier for the Swedes and Norwegians, who had less of a notion of nationality than the Irish, to create nationality enclaves, because the Irish were in the city and the Swedes and Norwegians were in the country. In Glazer's words, "We can, I think, conclude that where these early immigrants were isolated and remained rural, they showed an amazing persistence in maintaining the old language, religion, and culture. . . . For those . . . in the cities . . . a shorter time sufficed to remove the language and culture they had brought with them."

Glazer observes that among more recent immigrants, there are large numbers of people who came from nations struggling to become states (Poles, Lithuanians, Slovaks, Croatians, Slovenians), or from states struggling to become nations (Italy and Turkey and Greece), as well as from areas outside these Western concepts (Syrians), and of course one group—the Jews—who fit appropriately into none of these state-nation categories. "The newcomers became nations in America," Glazer points out quite succinctly; and he quotes with approval the insight of Max Ascoli, "They became Americans before they ever were Italians."

In two remarkable paragraphs, Glazer describes the astonishing phenomenon of the emergence of European "nations" in the American environment.

. . . Indeed, the effort of creating a national language, a task which the Western European nations had accomplished centuries before, was considerably facilitated for these Eastern peoples by American emigration. The coming together in American cities of people of various villages, speaking various dialects required the creation of a common language, understood by all. The first newspaper in the Lithuanian language was published in this country, not in Lithuania. The urbanization of many east European peoples occurred in America, not in Europe, and the effects of urbanization, its breaking down of local variation, its creation of some common denominator of nationality, its replacement of the subideological feelings of villagers with a variety of modern ideologies—these effects, all significant in making the east European peoples nations, were in large measure first displayed among them here in America. The Erse [Gaelic] revival began in Boston, and the nation of Czechoslovakia was launched at a meeting in Pittsburgh. And all this should not surprise us too much when we realize that some European areas were so depopulated that the numbers of immigrants and their descendants in America sometimes equaled or surpassed those who were left behind.

If nations like Czechoslovakia were in large measure created here in America, other immigrants were to discover in coming to America that they had left nations behind—nations in which they had had no part at home. Thus, the American relatives of southern Italians (to whom, as Ignazio Silone and Carlo Levi describe them, the Ethiopian war meant nothing more than another affliction visited upon them by the alien government of the North) became Italian patriots in America, supporting here the war to which they would have been indifferent at home.

. . . America's ethnic groups are rooted only very partially in the European preimmigrant experience, and have been shaped to a very great extent, however differentially for different groups, by the American experience. Glazer is quite right in saying that the Italo-Americans are very different from the Italo-Italians, and I can testify from personal experience that while the Irish-Irish and the American-Irish are in some respects similar, they are also very different. But this does not mean that American-Irish are about to become indistinguishable from American- Italians.

The ethnic group in this perspective is a combination of European cultural background, American acculturation experience (different for different groups), and political, social and economic common interest. Not merely do different origins produce cultural differences; the different experiences in America reinforce the old differences and create new ones. The Kennedy Administration was, one supposes, quite different from the administration of Sean Lynch in Dublin, but it is also very different from a WASP Administration in this country, or the kind of Administration we will have when finally Americans get around to electing a Jewish President.

There are a number of reasons why intensive study of

American ethnic groups is long overdue. First of all, as we pointed out earlier, the wandering of the nations which has produced the United States of America is one of the most extraordinary social phenomena in the whole history of mankind. It provides us with a marvelous laboratory for the study of human relationships. What is there, precisely, in presumed common origin that attracts us to others of similar origin and repels us from those of different origins? Ethnic interaction and conflict in American society can tell us many things about human relationships that we are only beginning to dimly understand.

Secondly, our society faces immediate social problems which cannot be solved unless we understand more about the operation of the ethnic factor. I need not look at the statistics . . . about Polish attitudes on racial questions to know that there is an acute problem in the relationship between Poles and blacks—at least one need not look at statistical tables if one lives in Chicago. Nor, if one lives in New York City, is it possible any longer to be unaware of the tension between Jews and blacks. If we understood more about how ethnic groups relate with one another, we might have some insights which would enable us to mitigate, if not eliminate, the dangerous tensions which threaten to tear apart our large cities.

Finally, it might be easier to understand the problems of the new immigrant groups if we were somewhat more aware of how older immigrant groups coped with their problems at a similar state in the acculturation process. I certainly do not want to subscribe to any interpretation of American racial problems which says that the blacks are just like any other ethnic immigrant group, and that their problems will be solved in the same way as the problems of the Irish or the Slovaks or the Italians or the Jews. For however degrading were the life conditions of the early white immigrants, they were at least not brought here as slaves nor kept in slavery or near-slavery for several hundred years. Nor are their skins a different color from that of other Americans. The combination of the slavery-serfdom experience and the difference in skin color (which, whether we liberals like it or not, still seems to be a universal human problem) puts the blacks at a much more serious disadvantage in acculturating to American society and obtaining their full rights than any previous group.

Nevertheless, there are certain similarities in the process through which all immigrant groups must pass in American society, and if we keep in mind that these are similarities and not exact identities, we can find them very illuminating. For example, there is, to my knowledge, not a single accusation that has been made by whites against American blacks that was not previously made against my Irish ancestors, with the possible exception that while blacks are accused of a high addiction to narcotics, the Irish were accused of an undue consumption of John Barleycorn. It was said of both groups that they were shiftless, irresponsible, pleasure-loving, violent, incapable of learning American ways, culturally inferior, too emotional religiously, and immoral (as proven by the high crime rates in their districts). The only basic difference that I can determine is that when the Irish rioted, they really did so in a big way. Nothing the blacks have yet done compares with—let us say—the antidraft riots of 1863 in New York. Similarly, when the Irish engaged in guerrilla warfare, they were far more ruthless and effective; the blacks have not yet, thank God, tried to match the Molly Maguires [a secret organization of miners in Pennsylvania in the 1870s].

Finally, one may also study ethnic groups simply because they are interesting, and because, of all the branches of social science, the study of ethnic groups generates more amusing stories (that are not pejorative to anyone) than any other branch of the discipline. Presumably American society needs all the humor it can get at the present time; within American society there is no segment more in need of laughter than the social sciences. But I wouldn't count on much laughter being tolerated there yet.

III. NATIVE AMERICANS: A SAD HISTORY, A NEW MILITANCY

EDITOR'S INTRODUCTION

We find that despite variances in attitudes amongst Indian people, . . . you have to realize we are all Indians, if that's even the right way to say it, in the sense that we are all here and that we can easily be classified and lumped into the category called Indians. What . . . I don't think people understand or appreciate readily is the fact that we are different, each of us. There are Mohawk people, there are Cheyenne people, there are Navajo people, Tlingit people, we are all different. We've had different experiences individually as of late, we've had different tribal experiences, we have different histories. And what people fail to realize, and I think even amongst ourselves we fail to realize this, is that we don't all think alike and we don't all act alike. —Michael Bush, a Caughnawaga Mohawk, executive director of American Indian Community House, Inc., New York City.

It is convenient to discuss Native Americans as one group, but American Indians do not constitute a single, unified ethnic grouping. There are literally hundreds of cultural and linguistic—that is, ethnic—distinctions, and the Navajo of Arizona have little in common with the Mohawks of New York. The Eskimos and Aleuts of Alaska are categorized as native Americans, but they are ethnically distinct from each other and from the Native Americans of the contiguous states as well. It is estimated that from 300 to 550 different languages were in use in North America before European colonization; about 150 are still spoken today.

While the details of Ingalik history differ from that of the Seminoles, there is a general history that all Indians have in common: an origin in the prehistoric past somewhere in northeast Asia (their immigration to the Western Hemisphere, over a period of thousands of years, was a movement so remote that it is lost in the strata of ancient rock or ice deposits) and confrontation with European explorers and

settlers in more recent centuries, followed by extreme social
and economic discrimination or victimization by the European Americans. They have, too, one significant culture trait
in common, often described as a "oneness with nature" or a
belief in the unity of all life.

For all native Americans, an integrated way of life was
irrevocably upset with the arrival of Europeans and their
expropriation of the land. The trauma of culture conflict had
its origins in the very first contacts between the Europeans,
who could not comprehend the Indians' attitude toward
land as an everlasting resource for common use, and the
Indians, who could not comprehend the notion of land as
private property that could be sold and lost forever.

Most estimates of Indian population at the time of the
European arrival hover around the one million mark. However, for a number of reasons it is believed likely that the
population might have been two or more times that. The
Europeans introduced not only conflicting ways of life but
decimating diseases, to which the native peoples had no resistance, and whole Indian populations were wiped out. By
1860 there were only about 340,000 Indians in the contiguous states and by 1910 some 220,000. Improvement in medical care even on the poorest reservations at about that time
resulted in a decline in the death rate, and the Indian population started to grow. The Census Bureau records that
from 1950 to 1970 this population more than doubled, from
357,000 to 793,000.

This rapid growth was undoubtedly a result of a continued high birth rate combined with the sharply lowered
mortality rate, but it may also have been significantly due
to a change in the Bureau's method of enumeration. Previously, Indian identity had been defined by the census-taker
and based on one fourth or more Indian "blood" (that is,
one Indian grandparent or two Indian great-grandparents);
enrollment in an agency or reservation; or the fact that an
individual was "regarded as an Indian" in his or her own
community. For the 1970 census, however, individuals were
asked to identify themselves and, perhaps because of heightened ethnic pride or increases in Federal benefits, many

more Indians than ever before were enumerated.

Demographically, 391,000 Indians, or almost half, were living in the west in 1970, especially in Oklahoma, Arizona, and California. The majority—437,000 or 55 percent—were rural; however, 308,000 or 39 percent lived in the larger urban areas.

Economically, Indians were more likely than any other racial or ethnic group to be unemployed and to have a family income below the poverty level. In 1970 they had an 11.2 percent unemployment rate (and that was before national employment figures plunged during the 1974–1975 recession). With a median family income in that year of $5,832.00, 33.3 percent of all Indian families were below poverty level.

This section opens with an extract from *Indian America,* by the noted writer Jamake Highwater. The excerpts briefly outline various facts of Indian life, including ethnic identity, language, legal problems, education, and the role of the Bureau of Indian Affairs.

Of all America's ethnic groups, Indians have been the most subject to false stereotyping. The second selection in this section is a survey of how Native Americans have fared in the hands of American writers. In the first part of this essay, books dealing accurately and sensitively with various facets of Native American history and culture are noted; in the second part, the sentimentality and false stereotypes that have been perpetuated in American literature (and film and television) are revealed and correctives suggested. Whether Indian or non-Indian, Americans are all the losers for being exposed to so much misinformation.

Partly because of improved education, and largely as a result of the general ethnic resurgence in the country as a whole, increased numbers of Indians have become determined to assert their rights in all spheres of life. But it is difficult to maintain a heritage of pride and freedom within the restrictions of reservation life, and until recently it has been next to impossible to retain traditions outside of an Indian community, especially when those traditions were being systematically devalued. The third article in this section is, on one level, an account of a lawyer's frustration in his attempt to bring legal services to an urban Indian population. On another level, however, it is a picture of Indian life in a modern city, an account of the dislocations experienced by a people who are political and economic refugees in a land that is their own.

The selections that follow are expressions of Indian identity and pride by Mifaunwy Shunatona Hines and Dawn Kathleen Good Elk, who, though they live in a large city, are determined to preserve the heritage of their people.

THE FACTS OF INDIAN LIFE [1]

Who Is an Indian?

It is not easy to explain specifically who is and who is not an Indian. Since there is no accepted legislative or judicial definition of an Indian, there is often no way of clearly determining if someone is or is not of Indian descent. The standard determination is based on whether an individual's family is known to Indians and lives among Indians on a reservation or in an Indian community.

Indians are quick to admit there is a certain prestige in being a "full blood," yet they also agree many important and famous Indians have been "half-breeds" (or even less than half). For census purposes, an Indian is identified on the basis of self-declaration. And if a person has not declared himself an Indian, he could still be counted as one if "he appeared to be a full-blooded American Indian or— if of mixed Indian and white blood—was enrolled on an Indian tribal or agency roll or was regarded as an Indian in the community in which he lived." . . .

The Tribes

"Tribe" originally meant a group of people bound together by ties of blood, speaking a common tongue, socially,

[1] From *Indian America*, by Jamake Highwater, author and journalist, of Blackfeet/Cherokee heritage, member of the White Buffalo Council, an intertribal organization. David McKay. '75. p 59-72. Copyright © 1975 by Fodor's Modern Guides, Inc. Reprinted by permission of the David McKay Company, Inc.

politically, and religiously organized to live together in a more or less defined territory.

When Indians were removed to reservations the word *tribe* came to have several different meanings. The BIA [US Bureau of Indian Affairs] considers 263 Indian tribes, bands, villages, Pueblos, and groups in the states other than Alaska eligible for federal aid. Additionally, 300 native Alaskan communities are served by the BIA, and 160 Indian communities, not directly under the federal jurisdiction of the BIA, are recognized by city, county, and state agencies.

An Indian becomes a member of a tribe by a variety of methods, by birth, by adoption, or by simply meeting membership requirements. The amount of Indian blood required varies from a trace to as much as one half, depending on the tribe. . . .

Language

Today almost all North American Indians speak English. In the Southwest, most also speak Spanish, although the historic wound left by the Spaniards has made it an unpopular language. In the Northeast, some tribes speak French as well as English.

Of Indian languages, only about 50 to 100 distinct forms remain from the approximately 300 different languages spoken in 1492 by the Indians living in what is now the United States. It is extremely difficult to translate from Indian to non-Indian tongues. This is often mirrored in the inaccurate pronunciation or meanings which come through the familiar translation of tribal and personal names. It's Chippewa vs. Ojibwa, but neither are accurate pronunciations of the original; Sitting Bull, Great Spirit, and Happy Hunting Ground fail to capture the original meanings of these names and word concepts. The grammar and semantics of Indian languages are at great variance with English. Even a rough approximation of meaning does not come through in translation.

Though some Indians refer to speaking "Indian," it is inaccurate, like referring to speaking "European."

Indians did not write before 1492. Tribes of the Great Lakes used picture writing, on birchbark instead of paper. This was largely for ritual records. The Walam Olum of the Delawares is an example of a famous ritual record, probably executed originally in pictographs cut into wood. Much later, in 1823, Sequoya, a Cherokee of mixed blood, produced an alphabet and written language. It was willingly learned by the tribe, and in 1828 a newspaper in Cherokee and English, *The Cherokee Phoenix,* was printed in Sequoya's syllabary.

It is difficult to learn an Indian language, and opportunities for formal training are rare. Some non-Indians have learned Indian languages through direct contact with the tribes over a period of time. Many traders, for example, have a basic knowledge of the languages of tribes with whom they deal. The same cannot be said of most officials of the BIA, who are usually as aloof, ethnocentric, and remote in their relations with Indians as the imperious Englishmen who regarded natives as dogs and wards. This is a great handicap to children from remote areas where English is not often spoken in the home. It greatly impairs basic education, making prospects for later academic training dim.

During the present parental generation's education, native language was not encouraged and many adults did not learn to speak their own languages. There is now a strong movement among the young, however, to revive all aspects of native culture, including language. Grandparents welcome this opportunity to share their heritage with their grandchildren. The old people remember painfully how their children, so eager for white middle-class status, were so anxious to jeer at and avoid Indian ways.

Only a few Indian languages have been translated phonetically, and most tribal newspapers are printed in English. There are, however, phonetic dictionaries and grammars designed for linguists and other specialists.

Indian pronunciations are extremely difficult for non-Indians. Furthermore, it would be almost as much of a task for an Iroquois to learn Navajo, for instance, as it would

PHILISTINISM AND THE NEGRO WRITER [1]

I went to a high school in New Jersey that was mainly attended by children of Italian parentage. It was about 98 percent white. At first there were only six Negroes, then twelve Negroes in the entire school. I wanted to see the other part of the world, so I went off to Howard University, a Negro school in Washington, D.C., and when I got to Howard, it shocked me into realizing the terrible sickness of my father. Later I came to understand a little more, but I hated my father in the sense of his not being a man. That is, because he was a person who did not have a college degree and who had to run an elevator, and I did not understand. Now, perhaps, I have come to understand why this occurs.

Howard University shocked me into realizing how desperately sick the Negro could be, how he could be led into self-destruction and how he would not realize that it was the society that had forced him into a great sickness. For instance, a story I told . . . which, I suppose, has become apocryphal, deals with life at Howard University. A student friend (he is now a lawyer in Philadelphia) and I were sitting on the campus studying one day and a watermelon truck passed, and I said, "Let's go buy a watermelon." So we bought this watermelon and went to sit on a bench in front of Douglas Hall. Tom Weaver, the boy I was with, had to go to class, and I was left there alone, sawing on the watermelon. The Dean of Men (who might still be the Dean of Men) came up to me and said, "What are you doing?" And I said, "Well, what do you mean? I'm just sitting here." And he said, "Why are you sitting there eating that watermelon?" I said, "Well, I don't know. I didn't know there was a reason for it, I'm just eating it." And he said, "Throw that away, this very instant." And I answered, "Well, sir, I can only throw half of it away, be-

[1] By LeRoi Jones (Imamu Amiri Baraka), black nationalist writer, educator, and activist. Chapter 4 of *Anger, and Beyond: The Negro Writer in the United States;* ed. by Herbert Hill. Harper. '66. p 51–61. Reprinted by permission.

cause I only own half. The other part of it is Mr. Weaver's and he's in class, so I have to wait until he comes out and gets it." The Dean, now quite agitated, replied with great emotion, "Do you realize you're sitting right in front of the highway where white people can see you? Do you realize that this school is the capstone of Negro higher education? Do you realize that you're compromising the Negro?" I was, of course, shocked. Later I had other experiences. For instance, the teacher who was in charge of the Music School there told Professor Sterling Brown, and some others who wanted to organize a jazz concert at Howard, that jazz never, never would be played in the Music and Art building. When they finally did let jazz in, it was Stan Kenton [white musician and orchestra leader]. These are all examples of how American society convinces the Negro that he is inferior, and then he starts conducting his life that way. . . .

The Negro writer is in a peculiar position, because if he is honest most of what he has seen and experienced in America will not flatter it. His vision and experience cannot be translated honestly into art by euphemism, and while this is true of any good writer in America, black or white, it is a little weirder for the Negro. Since if he is writing about his own life and his own experience, his writing must be separate, not only because of the intellectual gulf that causes any serious man to be estranged from the mainstream of American life but because of the social and cultural estrangement from that mainstream that has characterized Negro life in America. I have always thought of writing as a moral art; that is, basically, I think of the artist as a moralist, as demanding a moral construct of the world, as asking for a cleaner vision of society, and always asking that, no matter what your response, it be, as Ezra Pound said, "new—that you make it new, that you respond newly and personally and singularly."

I once wrote an essay called "The Myth of Negro Literature," which was published in a rather weird form in the *Saturday Review,* and the point I tried to make there was that, until quite recently, most of what could be called the Negro's formal attempt at "high art" was found in his music, and one of the reasons I gave was that it was only in music that the Negro did not have to respect the tradition outside of his own feelings—that is, he could play what he felt and not try to make it seem like something alien to his feelings, something outside of his experience. In most cases the Negro writers who usually wanted to pursue what "they" classify as "high art" were necessarily middle-class Negroes, and the art that these middle-class Negroes made tended to be an art that was, at best, an imitation of what can only be described as white middle-class literature, the popular fiction that was usually about tired white lives. The Negro writer who duplicated these tired white lives was only painting them black. Therefore he was saying essentially nothing about the Negro except that he had been desperately oppressed—so oppressed that he could not even remember his own separate experience.

Even so fine a writer as Charles W. Chestnutt, one of the earlier black writers, had to "cop out," as they say, by being a "refined Afro-American." He could not have just any sensibility. Not just any functioning intelligence that white America could recognize as being valid, as being some kind of intellectual commentary on the period or the society and the culture. . . .

So the Negro finds himself in a very weird position, that is, to be of this country but to have a culture—and it is a culture, because culture is simply the way people live, and it is reinforced by memory—to have a culture which is essentially an adjunct, separate from the mainstream of American life. The Negro either must assume culture properties that are not emotionally his own, in order to have a go at the mainstream of white America, or develop a literature (and stance) that seeks to identify and delineate the slave, the black man—the man who remains separated from the mainstream. This at least has the validity of separating oneself emotionally and, finally, intellectually from what turns out to be only mediocrity, even if it's well paid.

Disassociation from the mainstream—that is, what is said to be real by the white American image makers—is a very great virtue. The fact that Negroes moved to the city starting at the beginning of the twentieth century and became lost in the city is symbolic for the writer, who can now become more nearly anonymous—that is, he can come from anyplace and be anybody. He doesn't have to be the landed gentry. He doesn't have to be the New England aristocracy, which made most of American literature. He can be, literally, any man in the kind of anonymous circumstances that only the city provides.

The Negro writer, the Negro artist has two problems. First of all, he's got to make a break with the urge to get into the mainstream. The Negro middle class realized that in a society where black is a liability, the coolest thing is not to be that, so the first thing the Negro writer has to say is, "Well, I am a Negro," which is a great, dramatic thing. To say that is to realize that it means not only some racial delineation but a responsibility to a specific and particular culture, one that can be talked about meaningfully, simply because it is a human experience—your human experience. If I say, "I am a black man. All my writing is done by a black man," whether I label each thing I write, "Written by a black man," it's still written by a black man, so that if I point out a bird, a black man has pointed out that bird, and it is the weight of that experience in me and the way I get it from where it is to you that says whether or not I am a writer. . . .

But Negro literature has always been, in America, direct social response, which is, I think, the best kind of literature. We must ask the Negro writer what are his influences, and then, does he refuse to be taken in by what goes down and around as being the most admirable qualities of American culture. For example, there are certain important men who nominated Leonard Bernstein for the Pulitzer Prize in music and did not even understand that the finest composer America has produced is Duke Ellington. But they cannot even understand what Duke Ellington is, what he

has been doing these many long years, and that is just sick.
It's sick and it's fantastic. It's fantastic, but that is what is
happening. We are labeled as not having contributed anything. And they keep on asking, "What has been the Negro's contribution to American culture?"

Well, what has it been? You think about that. What has
it been? We've lived here, which is what everyone else has
done, and we have memories of our particular and specific
ways of living here, and that is valuable as a statement not
only about this place but about the nature of the world.
When I say social art, I mean not only art that is art by
anyone's definition but art that will tell you how man lives,
or, at least, how he wanted to live. In some black people's
haste to get into straight-up America it has come to the
idiocy of someone's perhaps appearing one day in *Ebony*
magazine for being the first Negro to drop an atomic
bomb—it goes to that kind of very dubious accomplishment, so that, as the man says, "The Negro has to be twice
as good to get ahead." So are we to drop two bombs?

The Souls of Black Folk, by Du Bois, and Langston
Hughes' book *Fine Clothes for the Jew* describe two different places in America—two different places in the emotional history of America. Both are equally valid, by virtue
of the precision of the telling, nothing else. It is the precision of the telling that demonstrates exactly what it is you
feel, by showing it rather than elaborating in some didactic
but finally noninstructive way—that is, by demonstrating
what art is supposed to do. So that I usually think of the
Harlem writers and Jean Toomer as doing this, despite the
social placement of this writing which white oriented
minds might make. But Toomer not in the same way, because Jean Toomer separated himself, first as an intellectual, as a middle-class intellectual, and then as a mystic.
Mysticism is, after all, the hard core of Negro culture, but
mysticism of another kind. Yes, mysticism, because the
spirit was always valuable—more valuable than *things* for
the Negro because he never had any thing. The religious
core of Negro culture still remains, is present, even in

[jazz musicians] Thelonious Monk or Ornette Coleman. They are trying to get at something which is finally spiritual and has to do with the transmitting of spirit rather than "writing a biography," which might be useful for some things, like trying to get a job.

If you think of W. E. B. Du Bois, Richard Wright, Jean Toomer, Langston Hughes, [Ralph] Ellison, [James] Baldwin, Chester Himes and all the others, if you think of these people you are forced to realize that they gave a top-level performance in the areas in which each functioned. The most meaningful book of social essays in the last decade is *Notes of a Native Son,* by Baldwin. The most finely constructed archetypal, mythological novel, utilizing perhaps a Kafkaesque sense of what the world really has become, is *Invisible Man,* by Ralph Ellison. The most completely valid social novels and social criticisms of South and North, nonurban and urban Negro life, are Wright's *Black Boy* and *Native Son.*

It's all there, even to the Raymond Chandler-Dashiell Hammett genre of the detective novel, in Chester Himes' *All Shot Up* or *The Crazy Kill* or *The Real Cool Killers* which are much more interesting, not only in regard to plot but also in terms of "place," a place wherein such a plot can find a natural existence. So that the Negro writer finally doesn't have to think about his "roots" even literarily, as being subject to some kind of derogatory statement —one has only to read the literature.

It is certainly impossible to understand the Civil War or the Reconstruction period without reading Du Bois about Reconstruction. It is impossible to understand the temperament of middle-class Negro life or the America that produces it without reading E. Franklin Frazier's *Black Bourgeoisie.*

The young Negro writer has all that great material, and that of our fathers and our grandfathers, and, in addition, has the just barely plumbed innards of his own cultural history. I am writing a novel now about something my grandmother told me, and the essential reality is this: One

day I ran into the house and said, "Grandmother, this boy
called me a nigger." She said, "Well, you are. You are. Nobody else is." The realization of that . . . *being* that nigger,
because that means you don't have the experience of being
what you *think* a nigger is, is extremely significant in many
ways. In jazz, people started talking about "funk," and the
white man had always said: "The Negro has a characteristic smell," but then the Negro takes that and turns the
term around, so that if you don't have that characteristic
smell, that funk, then the music, or what you are, is not
valuable. The very tools the white man gave the Negro are
suddenly used against him. These very weapons he has
given us.

And now we find, indeed, they are very valuable. . . .
Behind American and contemporary culture, in every way
that has meaning, there is the Black experience. It has become absolutely valuable for the black man to realize that
he exists and that his experience is as valid as any other.
My own direction is always toward spirit, which is the only
thing I admit as being real. I say, "Where am I? Who am
I? What's happening? Who are all these others?" And relate it to me.

So that if T. S. Eliot says something about the essential
strength of language as image, I take it to mean me. If
Pound says something about image as emotional and intellectual complex, I take it to mean me. If Apollinaire
[French poet, novelist, and essayist] says something about
space-time relationship or sense-drama or philosophical ab-
stracts, that is my reality. As, for instance, the idea of Christ
as an airplane pilot—I take it to mean me, something that
I can use, where I am, in my ghetto or outside of that
ghetto, but available as air is, or love is. It's there. You
know it. . . .

The writers in the ghetto will write about ghetto life
and the Negroes who find themselves outside of the ghetto
will go where art is and try to do it that way. Whatever the
expression and the experiences available, wherever we are,
our most important obligation is to tell it all exactly as it is.

FAMILY CHRONICLE [2]

When Alex Haley was growing up in Tennessee during the 1920s, his grandmother used to entertain him with stories about his ancestors. Her recital went all the way back to the days before the American Revolution, to the time when a man she called "the African" had been brought aboard a slave ship to a place she pronounced "Naplis." According to family tradition, this African forebear had called himself "Kin-tay," but the Virginia planter who purchased him renamed him "Toby." In a fourth unsuccessful attempt to escape, he was trapped by professional slave-catchers, who mutilated his foot so that he would never run away again. He mated with another slave, "Bell, the big-house cook," and they had a daughter called Kizzy. To this little girl Kin-tay told the story of how the slave traders had captured him when he strayed from his African village into the forest, and he drilled into her memory the words in his native tongue for half a dozen familiar objects, such as a guitar. When Kizzy was sixteen, family lore continued, she was sold to a small planter in North Carolina, by whom she bore a child called George. To this son she passed along what she could remember of her father's history. He transmitted the tradition to his children, and they in turn related the family history to their offspring, one of whom was Haley's grandmother. The stories that she told Haley, then, were part of an oral history that reached back seven generations—a period longer than the national history of the United States.

A journalist, Haley began thinking about the significance of this family lore when he started using tape recordings to prepare a biographical sketch of the jazz trumpeter, Miles Davis. Work on the book that was published as *The Autobiography of Malcolm X* strengthened his interest in oral history and also turned his attention to the African heritage

[2] Review of Alex Haley's *Roots: The Saga of an American Family*, by David Herbert Donald, Charles Warren Professor of American History, Harvard University; Pulitzer-prize-winning author; historian and educator. *Commentary.* 62:70+. D. '76. Reprinted from *Commentary* by permission; copyright © 1976 by the American Jewish Committee.

of American blacks. He began to check and verify what he could of his family history. After repeated failures, he finally succeeded in having the handful of African words that had been passed along, with some distortion, through seven generations identified as Mandinka, a language spoken along the Gambia River. On a trip to Gambia he learned of a village named "Kinte-Kunda," which sounded close to the name *Kin-tay* of his ancestor, and he was told of the legendary *griots,* very old men living in the backcountry who were walking encyclopedias of local history. At the village of Juffure the *griot* recited for Haley the complex history of the Kinte clan, including that of Omoro Kinte, whose oldest son, Kunta, born about 1750, "went away from his village to chop wood . . . and he was never seen again."

Convinced that he had identified "the African," about whom his grandmother had spoken, Haley searched through shipping records in London and Annapolis to trace Kunta Kinte's arrival in America in 1767 and his sale to the Waller family of Spotsylvania County, Virginia. After that link was established, his job was largely a matter of working through census records to trace the family's migrations from Virginia to North Carolina and, after emancipation, to Tennessee. *Roots* is Haley's account of seven generations of his family, from Africa to America, from freedom to slavery and on to freedom again.

As the reconstruction of a genealogy, Haley's book is a *tour de force.* Like Herbert G. Gutman's recently published *The Black Family in Slavery and Freedom,* it reminds us how even in appallingly adverse circumstances blacks often maintained, through oral traditions, a full account of their lineage and a proper sense of their individual identities. Skillfully, Haley checked his oral history against surviving written documents, and the family tree that he has outlined seems not just plausible but authentic. It is easy to accept Haley's statement: "To the best of my knowledge and of my effort, every lineage statement within *Roots* is from either my African or American families' carefully preserved oral history, much of which I have been able conventionally to corroborate with documents."

(Since Haley has been so successful in tracing his genealogy, perhaps a word of warning ought to be inserted for others who may be tempted to emulate him. Very few Americans, white or black, can hope to duplicate his triumph. Among American Negroes, the experience of Kunta Kinte, transported directly from Africa to British North America, was unusual. According to Philip D. Curtin's authoritative study of the Atlantic slave trade, fewer than 6 percent of all slaves brought to America in the eighteenth century came immediately to the British colonies on the continent. Most tobacco and rice planters preferred slaves who were "seasoned"—i.e., who had spent at least a year in the Caribbean, adapting to the climate and the work habits of the New World. It would be virtually impossible to trace a slave who was brought from Africa to Jamaica, then sold, say, in Barbados, and later shipped to South Carolina. Haley's family was also exceptional in the precision of its oral tradition. Finally, it was a combination of persistence and good luck that enabled Haley to link up his American and African oral histories and to corroborate key facts from written documents.)

Only the final twenty pages of *Roots* recount Haley's efforts to trace his family's history; the rest of this very long book is an imaginative account of how he believes his ancestors must have lived and acted. Haley admits: ". . . by far most of the dialogue and most of the incidents are of necessity a novelized amalgam of what I *know* took place together with what my researching led me to plausibly *feel* took place." *Roots* is, then, primarily a work of historical fiction, using the names of actual persons who were Haley's ancestors. Readers should not expect to find in these pages an accurate history of Haley's family, any more than they would look for a factually complete account of the Civil War in Stephen Vincent Benét's *John Brown's Body*. In a work of this sort it is enough to have a high level of historical plausibility coupled with enough literary skill to make the characters credible.

By this standard, parts of *Roots* come off very well. Since

I am not an Africanist, I cannot judge the historical ac-
curacy of Haley's reconstruction of Kunta Kinte's boyhood
in an eighteenth century Mandinka village. Perhaps for this
reason I found this section of *Roots* both imaginative and
persuasive. My colleagues who do know African history
warn that Haley tends to romanticize the beauties and com-
forts of primitive society, and I suspect that had Haley's
African safari lasted longer he might have written more
about the dirt, the discomfort, and the danger of life along
the Gambia. Haley's account of the Middle Passage—the
dreaded voyage from Africa to America—is also a convincing
recreation of that horror. There is no way of knowing
whether the Lord Ligonier, on which Kunta Kinte sailed,
was actually a vessel managed with such singular bestiality;
but Haley's account of the crowding, the stench, the brutality, and the disease on such ships jibes with other accounts
of the Atlantic slave trade.

Once Haley gets Kunta to America, however, the historical plausibility of his story begins to deteriorate. On
page after page there are factual errors as well as distortions.
No one of these in itself is weighty, but cumulatively they
create disbelief. For instance, Haley says that Kunta was
sold for eight hundred and fifty dollars in 1768. Perhaps it
does not matter much that his price would probably have
been set in pounds, shillings, and pence (though Spanish
dollars were sometimes used in local transactions), but it
is troubling that the alleged price is nearly three times what
Virginia planters were then paying for prime field hands
—unskilled but able-bodied young slave men who, unlike
Kunta, had already been seasoned. Bought by a Virginian,
Kunta is promptly set to work "hoeing the grass from
around the waist-high cotton"—though virtually no cotton
was grown in British North America in these decades before
the invention of the cotton gin. From a fellow slave Kunta
hears of "real big plantations with fifty or a hunerd slaves
[along] . . . the river bottoms like in Louisiana, Miss'ippi,
an' Alabama"—at a time when the Spanish owned Louisiana, and Alabama and Mississippi were populated only by
Indians. Similarly in 1790, a slave friend tells Kunta about

the rich lands of "de Yazoo Miss'ippi" and "dat black belt of Alabama, South Ca'lina, and Geo'gia"—thus anticipating patterns of settlement that were not to occur for at least a quarter of a century.

The most serious historical blunder in *Roots* concerns Kunta's grandson George—called "Chicken George" because of his skill in training gamecocks. In the 1850s when George's master loses a disastrous wager on his birds, he pays his debt by giving his slave to a visiting Englishman, who takes him to Britain for five years to train fighting cocks there. Despite Lord Mansfield's 1772 ruling in the Somersett case, announcing that once a slave set foot on British soil he became free, Haley has George remain a slave to the British lord. Sent back to America in 1860, George continues a slave, even though he stops off in New York, where the personal liberty laws would certainly have guaranteed his freedom, and he returns docilely to the South to entreat his master for liberty.

The point should be obvious: whatever Mr. Haley may know about Africa, he simply has not done enough reading about the South, about slavery, about American agriculture —to say nothing about general American history—to give his novel a convincing background.

Nor has Haley mastered the literary technique of historical fiction. Perhaps it does not make much difference that his characters are one-dimensional and wooden, for psychological subtlety can be as distracting in a historical novel as in a detective story. But it is awkward that the only way Haley can devise to introduce chronology is to have house slaves rush down to the quarters announcing the latest big-house gossip about Toussaint L'Ouverture, Nat Turner, John Brown, and the Emancipation Proclamation. It is awkward, too, that Haley has written most of *Roots* in heavy dialect. Not since Joel Chandler Harris [author of Uncle Remus books] has a writer had so many characters saying things like: "Less'n you niggers pick dis fiel' o' cotton clean fo' dat sun set, y'all ain't goin' git no mo' rations to eat."

Indeed, Haley's fictional technique closely resembles that

of Harris and other such late nineteenth century southern historical romancers as Thomas Nelson Page, Mary Johnston, and James Lane Allen, and *Roots* should be read as a continuation of this hoary tradition—but with the racial signs reversed. In Haley's novel it is a black family of noble lineage, rather than a white one, that is spirited off to adventures in America. In *Roots* it is the blacks who exhibit diligence, loyalty, truth, honor, and a fierce spirit of stubborn independence, even though they are surrounded by degraded, disgusting whites. In conventional southern historical fiction the worst thing that can happen to a white family is to have an admixture of Negro blood; in *Roots* the blacks fear the taint of white blood that would contaminate their pure African heritage. Just as traditional southern white historical novelists wrote of "darkeys" instead of Negroes, so Haley can hardly bring himself to speak of whites but refers to them throughout as "toubob"—presumably a word of African origin. And finally, just as in the conventional southern historical romance of the 1880s, Haley's family emerges from its trials unscathed, or rather ennobled, and at the end its members live happily and prosperously ever afterward.

Since we are all used to making allowances for the white racism that permeates so many nineteenth century historical novels, there is no special reason why we should not be equally resigned to the black racism in Haley's story. The problem, however, is that Haley's racism leads to an unfortunate distortion of his family's history. Admitting embarrassment that he himself is of mixed blood and feeling humiliated in the presence of truly black Africans, Haley is uncomfortable in dealing with the history of his family during the past hundred years, because that history is one of people with mixed blood who accepted, emulated, and excelled in the white American world. He prefers the story of his legendary, almost mythical, African ancestors to the fully documented history of his family since the Civil War. Only in the sketchiest outline does he tell us of the migration of that family as a unit to Tennessee, of their creation of a vigorous and prosperous new black community, of their economic success when one member became the owner of a large, well-managed lumber store, patronized by whites and blacks alike, so that members of the next generation could secure college educations. This is the real story of Haley's family, a typically American success story. That story of triumph over adversity would have been far more inspiring, as well as far more historically accurate, than any romanticized account of African ancestors.

ANNUAL PROGRESS REPORT: 1977 [3]

As the nation moved into its third century, blacks continued to find their horizons artificially limited and their mobility restricted through poverty and powerlessness in a society of plenty. Gains they had won from a decade of civil rights activity continued to erode in the face of mounting pressures from whites convinced that blacks had gained too much and whites had become victims of "reverse discrimination." For many blacks, the ever-smiling President Jimmy Carter was a glimmer of hope with his Lyndon B. Johnson-like promises of a fair and equitable government and his pledges of sensitivity to the poor and the black. Early on, Carter helped heal a divided nation's wounds by deflating the "imperial presidency," by reaching out to his fellow citizens, and by drafting an amnesty program that sought to relegate Vietnam's horrors to dim memory. He also inspired blacks and other Americans by stressing the importance of human rights in a world which flaunted them, and by pursuing an African policy that treats black Africa's aspirations with respect and encouragement for the first time in the nation's history. But whatever hope was aroused by these and other accomplishments gradually gave way to despair for many of Carter's black supporters. And so by mid-year they were agreeing with the National Urban League's Ver-

[3] From "1977: Year of Hope and Despair," by Alex Poinsett, a senior staff editor. *Ebony*. 33:24–5. Ja. '78. Reprinted by permission of Johnson Publishing Company. © 1978 by *Ebony* magazine.

non E. Jordan that an unexpectedly conservative Carter Administration had neglected them.

The Administration [charged Jordan in a blistering keynote address at the 1977 Urban League convention] has formulated a new foreign policy, a new defense policy and a new energy policy. But it has not adequately addressed itself to a new domestic policy. We have no full employment policy. We have no welfare reform policy. We have no national health policy. We have no urban revitalization policy. We have no aggressive affirmative action policy. We have no national solution to the grinding problems of poverty and discrimination.

Unemployment

While all of these problems continued to devastate black America, unemployment was easily the most urgent, peaking at the 14 percent rate reached during the 1975 recession. The official number of unemployed blacks remained the record high of 1.5 million. And when the Urban League's "hidden unemployed" (that is, discouraged workers, etc.) were included, actual black unemployment soared to more than three million in 1977 or one out of every four black workers. Worse still, the rate for black young people hovered between 44 and 60 percent (again depending on whether estimates came from the US Labor Department or the Urban League), despite the highest expenditure in history on summer job programs. Not fully grasping black America's crisis, President Carter's immediate response was to ask Labor Secretary Ray Marshall and Budget Director Charles L. Schultze to report to him reasons why black workers had been hit so hard.

But black economists and social workers for years have been pointing to institutionalized racism, the flow of jobs away from central cities, the decrease in the number of low-paying jobs and particularly the crippling impact of recent recessions as reasons why the black unemployment rate has been going upward steadily. Studies by the University of Pennsylvania's Dr. Bernard E. Anderson show that since 1968—the best post–World War II year for blacks—blacks bore almost the entire brunt of unemployment in the 1969-

to-1971 recession and had not yet recovered when they were hit by the even more seriously eroded economy of 1973 to 1975. As a result, Dr. Anderson reports, there is, on the one hand, a relative worsening of the position of blacks as a whole and, on the other hand, a worsening within the black community between college graduates, white-collar people and workers with great seniority on one side and the remainder of the black labor force on the other. While the first group has done relatively well over the past ten years, the other has been relatively untouched by the civil rights movement or the various poverty programs.

Thus the coalition of blacks, organized labor and other liberal groups responsible for President Carter's election pressed for passage of the Humphrey-Hawkins Full Employment Bill. However, it was far from clear to Robert S. Browne, director of the Black Economic Research Center, that sustained full employment would be achievable without a significant evolution away from the free enterprise ethic, that is, without "a degree of economic planning to which Americans are unaccustomed; some degree of mandatory job assignments; government enterprise in areas traditionally felt to be the preserve of private enterprise; and at least some limited control over wages and prices." Browne contended that the American economy, left to itself, is not going to solve the problem of black unemployment nor will the various income-maintenance and welfare-reform proposals. Meanwhile, the Census Bureau estimated that of 24.9 million people classified as poor (income under $5,815 for a nonfarm family of four) about 7.6 million were black, up 50,000 since 1975.

WHITHER INTEGRATION? [4]

Writing at the turn of the twentieth century, W. E. B. Du Bois argued, in his penetrating essays *The Souls of Black*

    [4] From an article by Martin Kilson, professor of government, Harvard University. *American Scholar*. 45:360–73. Summer '76. Reprinted from *The American Scholar*, Volume 45, Number 3, Summer 1976. Copyright © 1976 by the United Chapters of Phi Beta Kappa. By permission of the publishers.

Folks, that the color line was and would remain the distinguishing feature of American civilization, for only in the United States could color or race be cause for gravely qualifying the status of any group. More acutely than any other figure in Negro life, Du Bois recognized that ultrastigmatization drastically modified American citizenship for Negroes, rendering millions upon millions of them vulnerable in every sphere of their existence: work, schooling, play, voting, associational life, et cetera. Indeed, part of the condition of life as a Negro was that life itself was subject to violation anywhere, at any time, at the hands of anyone, through rigged judicial process, lynching, riot, police brutality. Existence for the Negro, as Du Bois correctly perceived it, was by definition dangerous. . . .

Negroes over the past two decades made serious political advances along with real economic and educational gains. Increases in the number of registered voters, actual voting, candidacies, and elected officials among Negroes have been nothing less than astonishing. For example, the registration of voting-age Negroes in the South increased from 5 percent in 1940 to 43 percent in 1964 and stands at 65 percent today. The character of Negro political leadership has likewise changed—from the civil rights leaders of the 1950s and early 1960s, whose influence has been largely moral, to a sizable class of elected black officials, whose influence rests upon institutionalized authority. These latter numbered less than 100 in 1960 but stand at roughly 4,000 today, constituting about 1 percent of all elected officials in America. And of course the total number of Negroes in politics is much larger than this (perhaps five times larger), for one must include in their ranks the thousands of Negroes recently appointed to political office. At the top of the list of appointed black politicians have been the first two Negro members of a federal cabinet—Dr. Robert Weaver, secretary of Housing and Urban Development under President Johnson, and William Coleman, secretary of Transportation under President Ford. It need hardly be added that these political advances have been made possible by the increasingly favorable attitude of whites in the postwar era toward including blacks in American life. White attitudes now favor even the election of a Negro vice-president and president—at least in polls some 76 percent of white voters have responded positively to this issue.

The euphoria over these heady gains, however, has now receded—as has much of the antiwhite, problack militancy that energized the millions of Negroes who helped to bring these advances about. In a word, the war is now over and the long, drab peace, with its concern about nuts-and-bolts American politics, has returned, but with this difference: the presence of Negroes at all levels of politics has now been institutionalized.

The question now is: To what use will these political gains be put? In the era in which we now live Negro political success will require highly imaginative leadership, for the substance of success will itself require a new phase of public policy innovation. No small task, this, since the national mood of the moment is at best skeptical and at worst implacably opposed to greater policy intervention in racial matters. Nonetheless, there are opportunities that might be favorably exploited by blacks and their new political leadership.

Taking the long view, however, the issue at the top of the political agenda for blacks is that of deploying black votes more carefully between the Democratic and Republican parties. The United States appears to be in an era of keenly contested presidential elections, tight races whose outcome figures to be close, with neither party likely to hold the White House for more than two consecutive terms. In this situation blacks cannot afford to nestle too comfortably in the embrace of one party (the Democratic) to the exclusion of the other (the Republican). The reason for this should be sufficiently clear: blacks have depended, and will continue to depend for a good while longer, upon government for the maintenance and extension of what gains they have made thus far in achieving parity with whites.

Negro voting must be intelligently diversified not only between the two major political parties but between black and white candidates. Throughout most of the 1960s a highly unified Negro voting bloc made much good sense; that was when large numbers of Negro candidacies first occurred and when the ability of Negro politicians to win office was still in doubt. But this situation no longer obtains, and other more varied uses for the vote are now in order. Opportunities here are plentiful. Nearly seventy congressional districts, for example, have a Negro voting-age population that comprises at least 25 percent of the total voting population. In such districts blacks would be remiss not to educate white politicians to their special needs. In some such districts this is already well under way. A prominent instance is that of Congressman Peter Rodino, the fourth-term incumbent of New Jersey's Eleventh Congressional District. A liberal best known for his leadership in the congressional hearings on the impeachment of Richard Nixon, Rodino has a constituency that includes the city of Newark, and 37 percent of his voters are black.

An important part of the task of informing white voters of the needs of blacks must be performed by those black politicians who have been able to win elections, through style and skill, in districts where the black vote is only minimal. The number of such Negro politicians is increasing, aided in part by the migration of blacks of all social classes to white suburbs and to smaller towns on the metropolitan fringe. (Four million Negroes now live in such suburbs and towns, as opposed to two million twenty years ago.) Senator Edward Brooke was the first Negro politician who owed his office to predominantly white voters, but there are others. In 1970 in California—the home state of Richard Nixon and Ronald Reagan—Wilson Riles, a Negro, was elected to the important office of superintendent of public instruction, defeating Max Rafferty, the conservative incumbent who ran a campaign emphasizing law and order. In 1973 Thomas Bradley, a Negro lawyer and former policeman, defeated another conservative white incumbent, Samuel Yorty, for the mayoralty of Los Angeles, a city whose Negro population is 12 percent. Moreover California and Colorado both have Negro lieutenant-governors, both elected in 1974, the

same year Wilson Riles was reelected California's superintendent of public instruction by a landslide.

Integration, in the wider sense in which I have been
discussing it here, is measurable by more than indicators of
social change. Cultural phenomena weigh heavily as well.
Many of the important cultural tendencies that are per-
tinent for racial integration had their origins in the counter-
culture and new styles of life that developed in the 1960s.
New cultural patterns and images related to racial matters
—particularly in the spheres of crossethnic marriage, popular culture, and the mass media—are now available to young
Americans, enabling fundamental change in the character
of American society.

The growth of cross-ethnic marriages, including interracial marriages, has been extraordinary. Until the 1960s,
most ethnic and religious groups could still boast extremely
high rates of endogamous marriage among their members.
Jews, for example, in the early 1960s recorded endogamous
marriages in the 90 percent range. Since 1965, however, between 30 and 46 percent of all Jewish marriages have been
to gentiles—one of the highest rates of exogamous marriage
recorded today, and this despite the efforts of Jewish organizations to reverse the trend. A similar situation exists
among other groups. In 1974, to cite another instance, nearly
40 percent of Japanese-American men married white American women. This is ironic when one considers the enormous press that ethnic pride and anti-melting-pot feelings
have received in America in recent years.

More to the point of racial integration, among Negroes
between 1960 and 1970 there were 64,789 black-white marriages—a 26 percent increase over the previous decade. Moreover, in the decade 1950-1960 there were for the first time
slightly more white male–black female marriages—25,913 of
them, a margin of 417 over black male–white female marriages. Although marriages of this character declined in
1960-1970, doubtless owing to the rise of virulent black militancy and the polarization of racial feeling that it brought
in its wake, such marriages, and interracial marriages in

general, are expected to increase markedly in the current decade. Experts agree that white male–black female marriages are an important index of fundamental change in the historical pattern of racial-caste labeling in America, and hence of the ultrastigmatization under which Negroes have lived.

Less easy to generalize about, but more pervasive, has been the increased presence of the Negro in popular culture, and in a new and different perspective. Rock music, for example, is the first successful mode of mass music—played and listened to by millions of white kids of all classes and ethnic groups and in all regions of the country—to contain a distinctly Negro cultural motif, albeit of lower-class Negro origin. Fundamental to what might be termed the *Negroness* of rock music is an expansive sense of abandon toward sensuality and sexual behavior, and, for better or worse, the sensual perception of white youth is increasingly shaped by this. Furthermore, although some white practitioners of rock music employ "white-rock" styles, most of them use "black-rock" styles—assimilating Negro speech modes and voice-tonal esthetics with surprising degrees of authenticity. No other generation of white popular musical artists, however much their music was earlier shaped by Negro forms, has shown the same degree of deference to Negroness. This new and unprecedented cultural diffusion between blacks and whites at least supports racial-caste dissolution; for if more whites—the young in particular—consider the Negro and his ethnicity an increasingly valid source of their own style, they might also begin to consider the Negro a legitimate member of American society.

In the media—television, textbooks, magazines, the press, movies—the old degrading image of the Negro as a superstitious, maniacally smiling, lazy coon that for so long dominated the view of the Negro in popular culture is just about dead. Television in particular has helped to effect this change. Millions of white families now see on their TV screens richly variegated portrayals of blacks in American life. For example, it would have been inconceivable to the early viewers of television after World War II that a generation later Negro models would be seen on television advertising products for highly personal use, such as cosmetics. It would of course be foolish to infer from this turnabout in the popular projection of the Negro that a radical change has occurred in the character of American race relations; yet it would be equally foolish to conclude that it is of no consequence whatever, save in the marketing of products in a capitalist economy. Indeed it is precisely because capitalism has endorsed this dramatic change in the popular image of blacks that I would expect its impact to be significant. Few things in American civilization succeed as thoroughly as capitalist-linked success, and however much one may bemoan this feature of our culture, it is a powerful institutionalizing force.

Over a generation ago, Gunnar Myrdal argued that the resolution of the "American Dilemma"—the nonfreedom of racial caste in a society whose primary premise was freedom itself—would occur when the American creed of equal opportunity for all individuals was extended to blacks and whites alike. Thus far the resolution of that dilemma, while well under way, has remained only partial. And it will continue to be so, Myrdal believes, until whites face up to the moral cowardice that lies at the heart of it.

Certainly the split personality, aided and abetted by moral confusion, that the average white displays in the process of extending the American creed is a continuing obstacle to racial integration. For example, in the area of sports—where Negroes now have a preponderant role after their fitful entry in the late 1940s and early 1950s—one finds much moral ambivalence in racial matters. Consider the city of Boston, where Irish youth cheer on the Celtics' Jojo White or Charlie Scott at the Boston Garden, or Jim Rice of the Red Sox at Fenway Park, but the next day shout "dirty nigger" at black children being bused into formerly white schools. Fortunately, most Negro leaders today are quite capable of open-mindedness toward this kind of ambivalence in the racial perceptions of the average white, who might be willing to change in one sphere of cultural and social life but in other spheres remains constrained by past habits and current anxieties. . . .

Finally, it has to be understood that integration is not a matter of interest exclusively to Negroes. The best of our leaders, black and white, have always understood it in a wider context—as a necessity for the nation at large. "I have a dream," announced Martin Luther King Jr., before he was brought down, and that dream, as he elaborated upon it, was not for Negroes alone but for every American. It was a dream of a society without hunger and without meanness, a society in which everyone could live his life to the best of his God-given limitations. That dream has seemed to fade in recent years. Ironically, in this, our bicentennial year, it has not been called forth as one might have expected it to have been. It remains the best dream we have, and the truest American vision.

V. THE NEW ETHNICITY

EDITOR'S INTRODUCTION

In the last decade there has been a resurgence of ethnic awareness on the part of numerous Americans. The pattern was set, in more ways than one, by the Black Power movement of the middle 1960s. For a variety of reasons, white Americans, including many whose European roots are several generations behind them, have decided to assert their distinctiveness instead of continuing to attempt to blend into the traditional American melting pot. The new ethnicity, as it has been called, is all the more striking because it contrasts so sharply with the prior efforts of immigrants to blend into the majority culture as soon and as much as possible.

In a sense the new ethnicity dates from its discovery by the scholars Daniel Patrick Moynihan (since 1977 a US Senator from New York) and Nathan Glazer, whose 1963 book *Beyond the Melting Pot* analyzed what had been going on all those years. The new ethnicity developed during the 1960s in response to a number of economic, political, and social factors. More than ten years after *Beyond the Melting Pot,* Glazer and Moynihan, in a *Commentary* article, observed that what was new about today's ethnicity was the shift "from an emphasis on culture, language, religion as such, to an emphasis on the economic and social interests of the members of the linguistic or religious group." Taking a broad view, they saw ethnicity as a phenomenon going beyond mere group survival, one that has become a "major trend of modern societies." Citing examples from Africa, Europe and the Far East, they pointed out that "ethnic identity has become more salient, ethnic self-assertion stronger, ethnic conflict more marked everywhere in the last twenty years."

America's new ethnics define themselves as white, predominantly of southern European and eastern European descent, largely clustered in blue-collar occupations, and for

the most part Catholic in religion. Michael Novak, a prominent activist-scholar and spokesman for this group, has referred to them, himself included, as PIGS—Poles, Italians,
Greeks, and Slavs. Novak, in *The Rise of the Unmeltable
Ethnics,* ascribed "the recent rise in ethnic assertion . . . to
the discrediting of traditional WASP styles in the face of
Vietnam, a revisionist history of Teutonic-Nordic prejudice
against other races and ethnic groups, and the failure in the
cities of WASP conceptions of social planning and social
reform." The day of the WASP, according to Novak, is
over. The ethnic revival is a protest against our increasingly
impersonal, fragmented, technological modern world, and
"a turn toward the organic networks of communal life: family, ethnic group, and voluntary association in primary
groups." In other words, ethnic identity is a way of recaptur-
ing the closeness of the small community and the extended
family, of meeting the basic human need for dependable
relationship. There is a distinction between "atomic" people, "those who know no neighborhood, who move a great
deal—the mobile ones, the swinging atoms, the true practitioners of the new religion"—and "network" people, "socially textured selves, not individuals," whose identity comprises "their relatives, their friends, their streets, their stores,
familiar smells and sights and sounds."

Today's increased emphasis on ethnic identity has been
criticized on a number of levels. Gunnar Myrdal, the Swedish economist, has protested that the new ethnicity is not a
peoples' movement; it is, rather, being led by established
intellectuals, "voluntary ethnics," who have neither studied
nor defined "those cultural traits to which they attach such
significance" and who do not really "reach the masses for
whom they pretend to speak." Myrdal puts his finger
squarely on the basic cause of dissatisfaction among America's ethnic groups: "It is poverty . . . not the lack of historical identity that holds American ethnics down."

Reprinted as the first article in this section is a brief
excerpt from the Glazer and Moynihan book in which the
authors conclude: "The point about the melting pot is that
it did not happen." In 1970 *Newsweek* surveyed the grow-

ing politicization of the new ethnics and the reasons for it;
the survey is the second selection in this section.

How does someone shift gears to become a new ethnic?
One answer can be found in the next excerpt, in which William V. D'Antonio, a sociologist, looks at his own Italian-
American family's history from immigration to education
and achievement; discusses the conflicts of "making it" in a
WASP world; and finally recounts the steps in his own full-
circle journey from belief in the necessity of assimilation
for his own and all ethnic (and racial) groups to his present
pluralistic outlook.

For Andrew M. Greeley, in the next article, ethnicity is
not a nostalgic harking back to a European past; it is, rather,
"a way of being American, a way of defining yourself into
the pluralistic culture which existed before you arrived."
From Greeley's point of view, "the black activism of the
1960's has legitimated . . . more explicit and conscious pride
in [ethnic] heritage" for other groups. Analyzing "the ethnic
miracle" of the southern European and eastern European
immigrants and their families, as exemplified in the successes of Chicago's Polish community, which went from
slum-dwelling poverty and degradation to suburban middle-
class comfort in half a century, Greeley points out that the
young immigrants displayed thrift and eagerness for hard
work, "Protestant," all-American virtues that led to their
success. Since most of these ethnics went to parochial schools,
the much-vaunted American public school could not have
been responsible for their achievement. Rather, he suggests,
the continuity of ethnic identity may well have been responsible—in particular, the family values transmitted during the earliest years of life.

Language is often the focal point in uneasy relationships
between schools and ethnic communities. Studies citing lack
of fluency in English as an impediment to educational
achievement have led some to urge that in areas heavily
populated by immigrant groups basic instruction be given
in native languages as well as in English, and such bilingual
school programs are now common across the country. But
many educators as well as lay citizens are convinced that bi-

lingual education is unsound and that it deprives children
of the thorough grasp of English they must acquire if they
are to succeed. The next selection, excerpted from *Editorial
Research Reports,* presents arguments for and against bilingual education and gives a brief account of dual language instruction in America.

A much broader concept of the function of schools
in our pluralistic country is presented in the sixth article in
this section, a discussion by Professor James A. Banks of the
historic role of American schools in transmitting ethnic
heritage. Banks advocates a more outreaching goal for education in a multicultural society, recommending that all
schools pay more attention to the experiences of all American ethnic groups, not only to the group that predominates
in a given neighborhood; this can be done, he argues, without yielding to separatist or racist extremism or losing sight
of the common or core values that constitute our national
heritage.

In the final article, the writer and educator Irving Howe,
often an advocate of ethnic awareness, warns against an
"uncritical glorification of ethnicity." Ethnic rediscovery
could lead back into provincialism, away from the international, broad outlook necessary in the modern world. Like
Myrdal, Howe sees today's problems as rooted in the inequities of economic class, high levels of unemployment,
and the dislocations and alienations of the decaying cities.
He urges all ethnic groups to retain identity but, at the
same time, move beyond the parochial to the larger concerns of the nation and the world we all inhabit.

BEYOND THE MELTING POT [1]

The idea of the melting pot is as old as the Republic.
"I could point out to you a family," wrote the naturalized

[1] From the book by Nathan Glazer, sociologist, author, professor of education
and social structure, Harvard University, and Daniel Patrick Moynihan, U.S. Senator from New York, former government official, author, professor of government,
Harvard University. *Beyond the Melting Pot.* MIT and Harvard University Press.
'63. p 288–91. Reprinted from *Beyond the Melting Pot,* by Nathan Glazer and
Daniel Patrick Moynihan by permission of The M.I.T. Press, Cambridge, Massachusetts. Copyright © 1963 by The Massachusetts Institute of Technology and the
President and Fellows of Harvard College.

New Yorker, M.-G. Jean de Crèvecœur, in 1782, "whose grandfather was an Englishman, whose wife was Dutch, whose son married a French woman, and whose present four sons have now four wives of different nations. *He* is an American, who leaving behind him all his ancient prejudices and manners, receives new ones from the new mode of life he has embraced. . . . Here individuals of all nations are melted into a new race of men. . . ." It was an idea close to the heart of the American self-image. But as a century passed, and the number of individuals and nations involved grew, the confidence that they could be fused together waned, and so also the conviction that it would be a good thing if they were to be. In 1882 the Chinese were excluded, and the first general immigration law was enacted. In a steady succession thereafter, new and more selective barriers were raised until, by the National Origins Act of 1924, the nation formally adopted the policy of using immigration to reinforce, rather than further to dilute, the racial stock of the early America.

This later process was well underway, had become in ways inexorable, when Israel Zangwill's play *The Melting Pot* was first performed in 1908. The play (quite a bad one) was an instant success. It ran for months on Broadway; its title was seized upon as a concise evocation of a profoundly significant American fact.

Behold David Quixano, the Russian Jewish immigrant—a "pogrom orphan"—escaped to New York City, exulting in the glory of his new country:

America is God's Crucible, the great Melting Pot where all the races of Europe are melting and reforming! Here you stand, good folk, think I, when I see them at Ellis Island, here you stand in your fifty groups with your fifty languages and histories, and your fifty blood hatreds and rivalries, but you won't be long like that, brothers, for these are the fires of God you've come to—these are the fires of God. A fig for your feuds and vendettas! German and Frenchman, Irishman and Englishman, Jews and Russians—into the Crucible with you all! God is making the American. . . .

The real American has not yet arrived. He is only in the Crucible, I tell you—he will be the fusion of all the races, the coming superman.

Yet looking back, it is possible to speculate that the response to *The Melting Pot* was as much one of relief as of affirmation: more a matter of reassurance that what had already taken place would turn out all right, rather than encouragement to carry on in the same direction.

Zangwill's hero throws himself into the amalgam process with the utmost energy; by curtainfall he has written his American symphony and won his Muscovite aristocrat: almost all concerned have been reconciled to the homogeneous future. Yet the play seems but little involved with American reality. It is a drama about Jewish separatism and Russian anti-Semitism, with a German concertmaster and an Irish maid thrown in for comic relief. Both protagonists are New Model Europeans of the time. Free thinkers and revolutionaries, it was doubtless in the power of such to merge. But neither of these doctrines was dominant among the ethnic groups of New York City in the 1900s, and in significant ways this became less so as time passed. Individuals, in very considerable numbers to be sure, broke out of their mold, but the groups remained. The experience of Zangwill's hero and heroine was *not* general. The point about the melting pot is that it did not happen.

Significantly, Zangwill was himself much involved in one of the more significant deterrents to the melting pot process. He was a Zionist. He gave more and more of his energy to this cause as time passed, and retreated from his earlier position on racial and religious mixture. Only eight years after the opening of *The Melting Pot* he was writing "It was vain for Paul to declare that there should be neither Jew nor Greek. Nature will return even if driven out with a pitchfork, still more if driven out with a dogma."

We may argue whether it was "nature" that returned to frustrate continually the imminent creation of a single American nationality. The fact is that in every generation, throughout the history of the American republic, the merging of the varying streams of population differentiated from one another by origin, religion, outlook has seemed to lie just ahead—a generation, perhaps, in the future. This continual deferral of the final smelting of the different ingre-

dients (or at least the different white ingredients) into a
seamless national web as is to be found in the major national states of Europe suggests that we must search for some
systematic and general causes for this American pattern of
subnationalities; that it is not the temporary upsetting inflow of new and unassimilated immigrants that creates a
pattern of ethnic groups within the nation, but rather some
central tendency in the national ethos which structures people, whether those coming in afresh or the descendants of
those who have been here for generations, into groups of
different status and character.

A RISING CRY: "ETHNIC POWER" [2]

Senator Edmund S. Muskie [Democrat, Maine] called it
"exactly what America must have if our democracy is to become more responsive to the people's real needs." Democratic chairman John G. Krupa of Lake County, Indiana,
branded it "a power grab . . . motivated by the godless,
atheistic forces of communism."

Muskie and Krupa, who are both of Polish descent, were
talking about the same thing—the Calumet Community Congress that was founded . . . by 950 delegates from 142
church, civic, fraternal and labor organizations in the grimy
Calumet industrial area of northern Indiana.

With its controversial launching at a sweaty, shirt-sleeved
convention in a high school gymnasium in Hammond, the
CCC became the newest example of a phenomenon that is
attracting attention in both Congress and in county court-
houses: alliances of white "ethnic power" groups designed
to give political clout to America's "forgotten man"—the
blue-collar worker of European extraction.

The first- and second-generation hyphenated Americans
have been spoken for in the past—by letterhead ethnic "con-
federations" and by such older, conservative umbrella organizations as the Polish American Congress, Inc. But the

[2] Article by Charles Roberts, former contributing editor. *Newsweek.* p 32–3+.
D. 21, '70. Copyright © 1970 by Newsweek, Inc. All Rights Reserved. Reprinted
by permission.

budding alliances of ethnics—inspired by liberal community organizers—have added a new dimension to the political landscape.

There are about 40 million ethnic Americans, concentrated in 58 northeastern and midwestern urban centers, and many of them are angry. As one former Hungarian freedom fighter from Cleveland put it, "I fought one revolution in 1956—and I'm ready to start another." They are squeezed by inflation, frightened by crime at their doorsteps, outraged by jokes and movies stereotyping them as hard-hat racists, and their homes and neighborhoods are threatened by bulldozers and blockbusters. What's more, they feel that they have been ignored by an Anglo-Saxon power structure and outshouted by a smaller, even more disadvantaged minority group—22 million Negroes. "Caught in the middle" is a phrase that is heard repeatedly from the Italians, Poles and Hungarians in Newark, Gary and Cleveland—all cities, incidentally, run by black mayors and WASP-controlled industries and scarred by racial disorders.

Taxes

The "nearly poor" in the $7,000 to $10,000 family-income bracket are not eligible for housing, job training, medical and legal-aid programs for the "real poor"—programs run by and for the blacks in many big cities. "As taxpayers, they support these programs with no visible relief—no visible share," a Labor Department study concluded . . . [in early 1970]. Tax reform has also eluded the ethnics, with bigger benefits going to the rich than to those in the lower brackets. For example, anyone earning more than $6,900 a year is denied a tax break for the expense of day child-care, making it difficult for wives to work. And in some states regressive tax laws penalize the lower brackets doubly—by overtaxing them and by providing funds for state universities to which they are less likely to be able to send their children.

Once too humble to complain and too proud to ask for help, the ethnics now complain that asking for help doesn't do any good. As a result, some of them are almost shouting.

"America is not a melting pot," says Barbara Mikulski, a tiny (4 feet 11 inches), thirty-four-year-old community college professor who speaks for Baltimore's Poles. "It is a sizzling cauldron for the ethnic American who feels that he has been politically extorted by both government and private enterprise . . . He is overtaxed and underserved at every level of government." [Mikulski was elected to Congress in 1976.—Ed.]

Together

Now, besides complaining, the ethnics are getting together. In ten cities—Boston, Providence, Newark, Philadelphia, Baltimore, Pittsburgh, Cleveland, Detroit, the Gary-Calumet area and Chicago—they are putting together, or have already forged, alliances to restore pride in their national origins and, more important, to make themselves heard on issues ranging from air pollution and inequitable taxes to garbage collection and zoning. "If we don't organize them, George Wallace or some other demagogue will," said a Calumet Community Congress worker in Gary. George Wallace carried Glen Park, a white ethnic enclave on the south side of Gary, decisively in Indiana's 1964 Democratic presidential primary.

The ethnics are being brought together, in many cases, by organizers who just a few years ago were working with blacks. "We are now about where the civil-rights movement was in 1960," says Monsignor Geno C. Baroni, a swarthy thirty-nine-year-old Italian immigrant miner's son who marched at Selma and worked in Washington's black ghetto before becoming director of program development for the US Catholic Conference's Task Force on Urban Problems.

Monsignor Baroni's title is a euphemism for his job: chief strategist of the nascent ethnic movement. The cigar-smoking activist priest maintains close contact with the ethnic organizers in all ten cities—whether they are mild-mannered Marianist Brothers, like twenty-six-year-old Joe McNeely of Baltimore's Southeast Community Organization (SECO), or tough graduates of radical [organizer] Saul Alinsky's Chicago training school, like thirty-year-old Jim

Wright, a 230-pound Mexican-American and former steel-worker who helped pull together the CCC.

Money

The Task Force on Urban Problems, based in Washington, has run seminars and supplied funds for many of the organizing efforts. ("After all, most ethnics are Catholics," says Monsignor Baroni.) Other money has come from Protestant denominations, however, as well as the American Jewish Committee and the Urban Coalition.

Their leaders deny that the ethnics are racist—or any more racist, anyway, than other whites—or that they want to "take anything" from the blacks. But among rank-and-file ethnics on the urban frontier you hear it both ways. "The blacks are getting it all," says a Cleveland Italian who was placed under a Negro foreman at his plant on the same day his son dropped out of John Hay High School after being beaten by blacks. "We've got to live together—there's no other way," says Leo Lulko, a Detroit Pole whose inner-city grocery has been looted once and robbed at gunpoint four times by Negroes. "These are good people," Lulko adds, recalling that his black customers protected his store with shotguns after its windows were smashed in the 1967 riots.

"If we are racist we learned it from the Anglo-Saxons who were here when we got here and have now moved to the suburbs," insists Stephen Adubado, a thirty-eight-year-old former civics teacher who is now building an organization called Displaced Ethnic Whites (DEW) in Newark. "Racism is a white thing, not an ethnic thing." Adubado, who broke the hold of two powerful bosses, ex-Mayor Hugh J. Addonizio and ex-Councilman Anthony Imperiale, on Newark's North Ward before turning to the ethnic movement, concedes "No. 1 priority" to the problems of the blacks. "But there are different kinds of cancer," he says. "Even though the white ethnic problem is less acute, it can still be terminal if it isn't attended to." His DEW, like Baltimore's SECO, is fighting to preserve old ethnic neighborhoods. "All that's left in Newark is the blacks, Puerto

Ricans and Italians," Adubado laments. "If you drive us
out, then you're going to have an all-black city."

Exodus

Racism aside, such urban experts as Richard J. Krickus
of Virginia's Mary Washington College cringe at the idea
of all-black cities. First, Krickus says, "the exodus of [white]
taxpayers deepens the plight of revenue-starved municipali-
ties unprepared to cope with a black underclass desperately
in need of welfare assistance, jobs, housing, better educational opportunities" and other services. Moreover, Krickus
contends, such a city "would magnify the hostility between
suburban whites and center-city blacks and Puerto Ricans,
and thus preclude any metropolitan approach to the myriad
problems that afflict urban America." Himself a thirty-four-
year-old Lithuanian migrant from Newark, Krickus con-
cludes: "The cost of solving America's urban problems will
become even more awesome if we ignore this crisis and fail
to take measures to contain white outmigration."

In most areas where the ethnics have organized—and all
are racial tinderboxes—their leaders are working with Negro
organizations to "depolarize" the cities. In Detroit, where
three out of five residents are either Negro or Polish, the
Black-Polish Conference, led by a Negro congressman, John
R. Conyers, and a Polish priest, the Reverend Daniel P.
Bogus, has already helped cool two tense situations—one
during last year's mayoral election (in which a Pole defeated
a Negro) and another after a Polish cop was shot dead outside a black church.

Now Representative Conyers goes to Pulaski Day dinners
and Father Bogus attends meetings of the Booker T. Washington Businessmen's Association. Both deny convincingly
that the conference has been used to advance the political
fortunes of the ambitious Conyers or any other black or
Polish politicians. "It's far too fragile a relationship for
that," says Conyers. "We are still in the process of melting
hostility." To avoid any appearance that the organization is
political or church-dominated, both Conyers and Father
Bogus plan to step down soon as chairmen.

In northern Indiana, the same church groups that helped form the CCC are now pushing the creation of a similar regional organization for blacks. The eventual aim of the groups, according to Lake County's Roman Catholic Bishop Andrew J. Grutka: to merge, or at least see that they "work together from a position of equality toward common goals."

Risk

Bishop Grutka, a sixty-two-year-old Slovak and an old friend of Saul Alinsky, a critic of the church, backed the CCC despite complaints from communicants about Alinsky's "radical" organizers. Now he is determined to stick by the Black Alliance, also being organized by an Alinsky alumnus. "I expect quite a bit of reaction," he says. "You've got to risk that in trying to change the status quo."

Given all the conflict and anxiety, large-scale cooperation between ethnic and black organizations is a long-shot prospect, to be sure. Such coalition would be a nightmare for politicians who are out of touch with their mixed constituencies, but they could be a boon to politicians with strong pulling power in Negro *and* working-class white wards. Perhaps that is one of the reasons that Senator Edward M. Kennedy [Democrat, Massachusetts] sent a warm wire to the CCC predicting that "perhaps in years to come the entire country will look to this [Calumet Community] Congress as proof that the democratic system can be made to respond to citizens united by common cause and concern."

CONFESSIONS OF A THIRD-GENERATION ITALIAN AMERICAN [3]

My grandparents on both sides came from Italy in the 1880s and 1890s from villages in Caserta and Benevento. They settled along with most of their relatives in New Haven, Connecticut, where my parents were born in 1899, one in an Italian neighborhood and the other in a predom-

[3] From an article by William V. D'Antonio, author and educator; chairman, department of sociology, University of Connecticut, Storrs. *Society.* 13:57–63. N. '75. Published by permission of Transaction, Inc., from *Society*, volume 13, number 1. Copyright © 1975 by Transaction, Inc.

inantly Irish one. My father graduated from New Haven
Hillhouse High School and my mother graduated from
night school with a degree in practical nursing. Both parents
valued education and pushed us hard (I am one of four
sons) to achieve in school. My father's entire job career was
in the United States Postal System, the last decades as superintendent of the Yale University Postal Station, an important influence on my life. I did not appreciate the fact at
the time (in fact, not until around 1962 when Professor
A.B. Hollingshead of Yale pointed it out to me), but my
family was among the early arrivals from Italy and we were
in the vanguard of third-generation Italian Americans.

In my youth, we lived within an extended family, Italian
American style. My paternal grandfather owned the three-
story house we lived in, and occupied the first floor with my
grandmother and unmarried aunts and uncles. An aunt and
uncle with four cousins lived on the second floor and we
lived on the third floor. All of my grandfather's married
children lived within walking distance, as did most of my
mother's family. Seeing and being with relatives was a daily
experience which was heightened on weekends and reached
a crescendo during the big holidays. On Easter and Christ-
mas especially, we could expect to see all of the paternal
relatives, and because of my mother's position as the eldest
child in her family, her relatives also gravitated toward our
house. . . .

The Neighborhood

We lived in a fringe neighborhood, working and lower
middle class, mostly two- and three-story houses that were
privately owned and frequently painted. The immediate
neighborhood was overwhelmingly Italian, with a few Irish
and one or two Polish families scattered within. (My father
reports that ours was the first Italian family to move into
the neighborhood, which was, in 1900, predominantly Irish.
It became Italian within twenty-five years.) The neighborhood was near areas that have long been associated with the
heart of Italian family life in New Haven, Wooster Square

and Grand Avenue, but our daily living patterns gradually took us away from those areas. For our neighborhood was also near Polish and German ones and also allowed us to interact in the solidly middle- and upper-middle-class neighborhoods then peopled largely by third- and fourth-generation Irish Americans. It was a comfortable neighborhood to grow up in, with lots of friends and relatives to play with, and, as long as we stayed within our boundaries, little trouble with outsiders.

Part of my growing up involved learning that there were Italians and Italians, that only Neapolitans could be trusted, that *i siciliani no sono cristiani, i calabresi sono capodosti* [The Sicilians are not Christians, the Calabrians are stubborn] and all northerners were stuck-ups. We had to watch out for the Jews, stay away from the Poles and recognize that the Irish were in control of things—but we would have our turn some day. The blacks must not have been a factor in the early days; I never heard anything about them. They lived in their neighborhood along Dixwell Avenue, at least until the expansion pressures during and after World War II. . . .

Americanization

For those who were in a position to benefit therefrom, the school was a good avenue for mobility. We were being taught by people who exemplified the middle-class Protestant values of American society and they did their job well. They felt a missionary zeal to Americanize us and were proud of their achievements.

High school was a mixed bag. Our parents urged us to think in terms of college and we signed up for the pre-college program. At that time, Hillhouse High School had a reputation for academic excellence, despite the rapidly changing nature of the student population. The largest group of students in the college prep program were Jewish, with an equal admixture of Italians and Irish, a smattering of other ethnics and a few WASPs; most of the WASPs attended New England's prestigious private schools.

High school did several things:

☐ Highlighted ethnicity. We had ethnic-oriented fraternities and sororities, dating was ethnic-oriented and cross-ethnic dating was a matter of family and peer discussion and censure. The WASPs had originated the system with their exclusive fraternities and sororities. The ethnics simply followed suit and established their own. In 1943 we broke new ground in intergroup relations by sponsoring a dance jointly between an Italian and a Jewish fraternity.

☐ Heightened awareness of status, power and class differentials, along with religious and ethnic differences. These differences were evident in dating, in high school politics, in what we learned about the groups that came from other parts of the city; they were increasingly evident in what we were learning about the larger community of New Haven. The question of race was not a factor in our lives in 1943.

☐ Fostered the assimilationist ethic at the same time it fostered ethnocentric pluralism. The message was clear: school was available to all those who wanted to get ahead. The teachers were there to help us on the way—as long as we followed their rules. They were believers in the system and so were we.

☐ Tended to obscure class and status divisions by focusing on ethnicity. Thus, for example, the members of the fraternity I belonged to came from families with income levels ranging from just above poverty to upper class. In this setting, the ethnic tie was more important than the class tie and this carried over into the dating patterns.

☐ Most important, Hillhouse High School made it possible for me to attend Yale University. Actually, my parents never talked about any place other than Yale, and my older brother and I both succeeded in winning scholarships to Yale. Of those who won scholarships to Yale that year (1943) from New Haven, four were of Irish backgrounds, five were Jewish and four were Italian, out of fifteen scholarships awarded. In some ways, we were the blacks and Puerto Ricans of that day.

Road to Assimilation

During the decade between 1943 and 1953 I found my-self increasingly absorbed into the mainstream of American life, embracing wholeheartedly the ideology of assimilation and individual achievement, and abashed by and ashamed of the ethnic struggles that seemed to absorb the energies of my elders. I was probably a typical example of the third-generation American who fulfilled the dreams of their parents, but caused them anguish by disavowing their ethnic ways.

My freshman year at Yale was a near disaster, socially and academically. I was unprepared for the level of work expected, mostly because I was not ready to cut myself off from the neighborhood gang and the high school fraternity gang. In their midst I was important, had achieved some-thing and yet my marginal status was like that of most others. At Yale I felt out of place and of course the fault was clearly mine. I did not know how to dress or act or how to study. While almost everyone else lived in one of those magnificent Yale buildings, I was a townie.

One interesting and, in retrospect, somewhat amusing attempt to compensate for social insecurity was my decision to join the Italian Junior League (IJL), a club composed of high school graduates, the poor people's imitation of the prestigious New Haven Junior League. While they had their own private club to meet in, we met at the YWCA. The IJL did provide an opportunity for social life with high school graduates, and for some of us it presented an opportunity for leadership training. We were not ready for the big time, but we did run an organization and we could pride ourselves on the success of our dances and big parties.

Then the navy intervened and altered my life experiences, to gradually wean me away from ethnic ties and to broaden my perspective of the world. Religion and class began to replace ethnicity as central concerns. More and more I tried to reconcile religious beliefs with secular knowledge and problems of peace and economic exploitation. The issue of race became important to me.

On my return to Yale, I studied Italian, but as a student

of language and not to rekindle ethnicity. Most of the students in the class had spent time in Italy, and talked knowingly about Firenze and the Ponte Vecchio. In some ways, I was probably quite visibly ethnic, a New Haven Italian with a Neapolitan accent who knew practically nothing about Italy, Italian opera or the like. In fact, I could not even speak Italian well, so attuned to American ways had my family life become.

A number of significant events occurred during my postwar years at Yale. We moved to a comfortable English-Tudor-style home outside New Haven near the Yale Bowl. We were finally free of my grandfather and the ethnic neighborhood, but not of family ties. My parents celebrated their move by frequent family picnics. For years our home was the center of extended family gatherings.

Italian Power

Meanwhile, Italian power had finally come to New Haven, first with the election of William Celentano on the Republican ticket, ending a fifty-year reign for the Irish. That was followed shortly by the election to Congress of Albert Cretella, also on the Republican ticket. Italians were deserting the Democratic party in large numbers to assert their desire for top political office. The major result, in terms of patronage, of these changes in fortune for my family was control of the New Haven Post Office. I found myself upset at the openness of the power play and the knowledge that key appointments would go to Italians, regardless of achievement, competitive examinations and the like. My father was upset with me for the silly notions I had about how the system was supposed to work.

The main source of family discontent centered around the first sociology course I decided to take, which was on race and nationality relations. It was taught by Raymond Kennedy, one of the most popular lecturers at Yale. He had a reputation for tearing apart the foibles of white ethnics and brazenly defending the cause of the Negroes. I found the course stimulating and exciting, and began to preach the cause of total assimilation and integration, which meant racial intermarriage. I reminded my family that there would be no Negro race in two hundred years because we would all become one great admixture. I assumed that this was what blacks also wanted. While I cheered on the cause of the blacks, I chided my family about the statistics showing Italians with higher rates of violence and rape than blacks.

Ethnic clubs like the Sons of Italy and Amici became very distasteful to me, as did the reality of ethnic politics. We should be assimilating, treating everyone as equals. Instead, we seemed to continue what were clearly now un-American patterns of behavior. I focused my attention increasingly on Latin American studies and Spanish, and on trying to develop a reasonable understanding of myself as a Catholic American, trying to prove I was as good an American as anyone else.

Through a series of fortuitous circumstances (upon graduation from Yale), I was offered a position as teacher of Spanish at the Loomis School in Windsor, Connecticut. Loomis was and is one of New England's prestigious prep schools. If I was the token Italian at Loomis, that fact went unnoted for the most part. It was the religious factor that mattered. Loomis had a distinctly Unitarian orientation and I found myself in regular conversation about Catholicism. While there were several other Catholics on the faculty, they did not discuss religion. Since I was eager to and felt increasingly comfortable in the discussions, a wide range of Protestant and agnostic faculty wanted to probe my Catholic beliefs.

In many ways, Loomis was the culmination of the assimilation process for me. After a bumpy first year, I found myself increasingly at home there. I was impressed by the emphasis on self-discipline, internal democracy and the like. The gospel of American democracy and the American dream was preached with great enthusiasm. To strive to achieve was the key. The school even had a regular guest speaker's program entitled "Loomis Learns from Leaders."

In 1950 I married a third-generation Italian whose father had achieved notable success as a small businessman in New Haven. He offered us a wedding reception at the New

Haven Lawn Club. With some concern about whether our relatives would be "comfortable" in the New Haven Club, we went ahead and had a very delightful, if somewhat non-ethnic, wedding with the wedding mass in St. Joseph's and the reception at the New Haven Lawn Club, thus presumably completing the assimilation process.

In 1954 I began work on my Ph.D., at Michigan State University, in sociology and anthropology. Throughout my years as a graduate student and until the mid-1960s, the most pressing ideological question I faced was how I could possibly be a sociologist and a practicing Catholic at the same time. On a theoretical level, I was taught to be value free, and that the proper model of society was built on concepts like integration, assimilation, equilibrium, order and functionalism.

For sixteen years I worked on and off along the United States-Mexican border, studying influentials, elites, business and politics, and the images which leaders had of each other. Early on I was aware of the plight of the Mexican Americans, but I understood their situation within an assimilation framework. Along with Julian Samora, the first Mexican American to earn a Ph.D. in sociology, I looked for evidence of the assimilation process at work; in 1962 we published an article on ethnic stratification in the Southwest, but our message was that through such vehicles as the Catholic Hospital, Mexican Americans were slowly but surely finding their place in American society. We found that their progress compared favorably with that of Italian Americans in New Haven, measured in terms of achievement in professional medical occupations. I was aware of the prejudice and discrimination from which Mexican Americans suffered in the Southwest, but felt certain that the assimilation process, which I thought had worked so well for the ethnics of the North, would surely be at work in places like El Paso.

Organizational Strength

As I moved away from social psychological to more strictly sociological concerns, I began to become aware of the differences that organizational strength made in the chances of individuals and groups. The Anglos were well organized; the Mexican Americans were not. I began to wonder if ethnic clubs were really all that bad. The Democratic party was weak in El Paso, there were no strong labor unions and ethnic clubs were lacking. Without organization, people had little political or other clout, and were not likely to improve their class and status positions. The word *chicano* was not in use then, for the brown power movement had not yet begun. . . .

Within the Catholic Church, Vatican II [Ecumenical Council, 1962-1965] was bringing new hope; I was now a member of the Notre Dame faculty and an increasing number of nonbelieving colleagues in the Midwest universities grudgingly conceded that perhaps I could be a Catholic and a sociologist after all. The birth control issue and population growth in Latin America occupied an increasing part of my time, as well as civil rights and the Great Society [program for economic and social reform put forth during the Administration of Lyndon B. Johnson]. Along with so many other white liberals, I joined the march for the civil rights of blacks.

The civil rights issue was and remains complex, an issue that I am not sure I fully understand to this day. In 1965 I was full of energy to implement both integration and the Great Society. By 1967, like many others, I was discouraged, and by 1969 I was ready to ask: What went wrong? . . .

We preached with a vengeance: we told white Catholic ethnics in the North that they could only be Christians if they accepted the blacks as brothers and sisters and living in the house next door. We mixed religion, class and ethnic factors—to our own downfall—and focused primarily on prejudice, as if personal prejudice were the chief cause of discrimination in society.

We became very unsociological, those of us who were sociologists and prointegrationists; we believed our own rhetoric about assimilation, consensus, equilibrium, the end of ideology and the like. We no longer saw white ethnics as we saw blacks or Puerto Ricans and chicanos. How could we? We believed that all whites had made it or were about to—at least all the whites who wanted to make it and who were willing to work.

But white ethnics had not made it out of their ghettoes, which were still meaningful communities to them. We discounted the values of that community life and the knowledge we should have had about the strength of their solidarity. We did not get the point of Glazer and Moynihan's book *Beyond the Melting Pot*. [For a brief excerpt see the first article in this section, above.]

Ideology and Social Reality

. . . In 1969 Daniel P. Moynihan was the commencement speaker at Notre Dame, and I was invited to be his host during his stay on campus. Since he was Nixon's urban adviser, some of us thought it an appropriate opportunity to invite him to a special gathering of social scientists to discuss an embryonic project we had in mind regarding blacks and small business. Moynihan was forthright—he told us to forget about studying the blacks and definitely not to waste any energy on blacks and small business. The Nixon Administration had already given up the idea of trying to make small business successes out of the black population. Instead, Moynihan urged us to return to the cities to study white ethnics. He assured us that emphasis was quickly switching to white ethnics, and we needed to know the meaning of the revitalization of white ethnicity. We were taken aback somewhat, gave some cursory discussion to his ideas, but were not ready to buy them.

By 1970 Representative Roman Pucinski was sponsoring the Ethnic Heritage Study Program in Congress, and we at Notre Dame had formulated a rough proposal for an ethnic studies program at the university to incorporate black studies with those of the white ethnics who had made up so much of Notre Dame history. Representative Pucinski heard about our effort, asked for support of his bill and gradually we were drawn into the realization of the strength of the white ethnic movement.

Return of the Ethnic

In 1971 I was invited to become head of the department of sociology at the University of Connecticut. At the same time, I was becoming more and more concerned about the ethnic factor in American life, and how it intertwined with class to present dangerous problems to the society. The move also provided the opportunity to work with several other sociologists and others at the university who were increasingly involved in ethnic studies. Most personally, it meant the opportunity to include the study of my own ethnic group in my research. I was no longer sure about the right solutions to our racial-ethnic problems, but fairly certain that there was something wrong with the whole idea of assimilation, and also that there was some relationship between that and the American value preference for individual achievement.

It seems increasingly clear that assimilation, both as theory and ideology, along with the ethic of individual achievement and equality of opportunity and the consensus model of American society are in need of revision, if not abandonment in favor of a more humanistic orientation. Many ethnics have been assimilated into American society, and many can say that the American success ethic worked for them. But that fact only obscures the social reality in which so many millions of ethnics still live. The assimilation-success ethic prevents us from understanding the meaning of the poverty, poor housing, poor educational opportunities, inadequate health care, degrading job situations and general insecurity in which so many people live. More than that, it prevents ethnics, black, brown and white, from appreciating the fact that there is no way out for so many millions of them.

What this ethic of assimilation-success does is to make us believe in the system as it is; those who do not make it, for whatever reason, are taught to blame themselves, rather than the system for their failure.

If assimilation, the melting pot and the success ethic have serious shortcomings, what are the alternatives? Ethnic pluralism can be a viable answer to assimilation and, as ideology, it can be developed to foster positive self-images while not denigrating outsiders.

I can relax now and look with satisfaction upon my family's struggle and upon their continuing identification as ethnics, if that is what they want. I do not have to worry if my mannerisms are not 100 percent American, nor if my family has learned all the "right ways" to do things. Mannerisms become alternatives, not preferred values.

My history did not begin with my assimilation into society, nor is it dependent solely upon my ability to see myself as somehow descended from the Pilgrim fathers. Ethnicity has been very important in my own life experience. I did not, as I had earlier thought, overcome it in the pursuit of assimilation and success. By appreciating our ethnic heritage, we can help insure that people develop a sense of self-worth without having to downgrade others. Ethnic groups are often the only organized groups within urban centers. What kinds of coalitions would they build if they enjoyed the organizational knowledge of business, political and other groups? They might well develop some new alternatives for confronting the persistent inequalities of American life, an effort worthy of support.

THE ETHNIC MIRACLE [4]

The neighborhood is a ten-square-block area with almost 14,000 people, an average of 39.8 inhabitants per acre—three times that of the most crowded portions of Tokyo, Calcutta, and many other Asian cities. One block contains 1,349 children. A third of the neighborhood's 771 buildings are built on "back lots" behind existing structures; the buildings are divided into 2,796 apartments, with a ratio of 3.7 rooms per apartment. More than three quarters of the apartments have less than 400 square feet. Tenants of the 556 basement apartments stand kneedeep in human excrement when even moderate rainstorms cause plumbing breakdowns. Garbage

[4] From an article by Andrew M. Greeley, program director, National Opinion Research Center. *Public Interest.* 45:20–36. Fall '76. Copyright © 1976 by National Affairs, Inc. Reprinted by permission.

disposal is a chronic problem—usually, trash is simply dumped in the narrow passageways between buildings. Nine thousand of the neighborhood's inhabitants use outdoor plumbing. The death rate is 37.2 per thousand per year.

These are the poorest of the poor people, making less than three quarters of the income of nonminority-group members in the same jobs. The rates of desertion, juvenile delinquency, mental disorder, and prostitution are the highest in the city here. Social disorganization in this neighborhood, according to all outside observers—even the sympathetic ones—is practically total and irredeemable.

Blacks? Latinos? Inhabitants of some Third World city? No—Poles in Chicago in 1920.

The neighborhood is still there. You drive in from O'Hare airport and see the towering spires of St. Mary of the Angels, St. Stanislaus Kostka, and Holy Trinity. If you turn off at Division Street you will see that the manure boxes are gone, and so are the backyard buildings, the outdoor plumbing, the sweatshops over the barns, the tuberculosis, the family disorganization, the violence, and the excessive death rates.

For the most part, the Poles are gone too. Some of them remain, sharing a much more pleasant (and brightly painted) neighborhood with Puerto Ricans. Where have the Poles gone? Farther northwest along Milwaukee Avenue, even out into the suburbs—they are now a prosperous middle class. How have they managed to make it, this most despised of all the white immigrant groups? It is no exaggeration to say that no one really knows, and that the success of the southern and eastern European immigrant groups who frantically crowded into the United States before the First World War is as unexplained as it is astonishing. Indeed, rather than to attempt an explanation, many Americans—including some from those very same ethnic groups—prefer to deny the phenomenon of ethnic success. [See "Ethnic Succession in America," in Section II, above.]

Yet the "ethnic miracle" is one of the most fascinating stories in the history of the United States, an American success story, an accomplishment of the "system" in spite of itself; and while the "ethnic miracle" does not necessarily provide a model for later groups (in fact, it almost certainly does not), it does offer insights into how American society works that social-policy-makers can ill afford to ignore.

The neighborhood I described is called the "Stanislowowo" after St. Stanislaus Kostka, its parish church. At one time, it was the largest Catholic parish in the world (forty thousand members) in the second largest Polish city in the world. . . .

There were no quotas, no affirmative action, no elaborate system of social services, and, heaven knows, no ethnic militancy (although it need not follow that there should not be these things for the more recent immigrants to the big cities of the United States). There was no talk of reparation, no sense of guilt, no feelings of compassion for these immigrants. The stupid, brutal, but pathetic heroes of Nelson Algren's novels were about as much as most Americans recognized; "Scarface" and "Little Caesar" of the motion pictures were taken to be typical of the Italians who got beyond street cleaning, ditch digging, garbage collection, and waiting on tables. It is safe to say that in the twentieth century, no urban immigrants have been so systematically hated and despised by the nation's cultural and intellectual elites. The stereotypes may be more sophisticated now, but they still portray the ethnics as hateful and despicable. Stanley Kowalski [the character portrayed by the young Marlon Brando in *A Streetcar Named Desire*] has been replaced by Don Corleone, but both still represent the white ethnic as a blue-collar, racist, hardhat, chauvinistic "hawk"—even though available statistical evidence does not support the myth of the Godfather or the bigot, and lends no credence to the ethnic joke.

Closely related to the thesis of the racial inferiority of the eastern and southern European immigrants was the theory of their cultural inferiority. "Social disorganization" was the explanation of the plight of the Stanislowowians offered by the "Chicago school" of sociology. The cultural values of the immigrants were not able to absorb the shock of the immigration experience and the resultant confrontation with the more "modern" values of the host society. . . . Fortunately for the ethnics, they stopped being poor before the reformers could set up high-rise public housing and dependency-producing welfare legislation to "undisorganize" them.

Across the Chicago River from "St. Stan's" is the infamous Cabrini-Green high-rise public housing project, one of the most evil things that good intentions have ever produced—a monstrosity that causes the very "social disorganization" it was designed to eliminate. . . . If contemporary welfare, urban renewal, and public housing legislation had existed a half century ago, the Poles might still be poor, and sociologists might still be writing books about how the Polish family structure—one of the strongest in America—is "disorganized."

One need not conclude that there ought to be no government intervention to help and protect the poor. On the contrary, the "ethnic miracle" might have happened more quickly if the government had intervened to prevent discrimination and to facilitate the rise out of poverty. But the "ethnic miracle" at least raises questions as to whether social legislation would be more effective if it were to respect the culture and family life of the poor and fight poverty directly, rather than with mostly useless attempts to correct "alienation" and "social disorganization." There obviously are individuals and families so badly traumatized by either poverty or misguided efforts to "unalienate" them (or combinations of both) that they cannot cope with problems or urban living without help from society. But the "ethnic miracle" suggests that such help should be aimed at making them think and act not like psychiatrically oriented social workers but rather like the more successful members of their own cultural community. . . .

Explanations for Success

The 1920s and 1930s were bad times for the immigrants and their children. The fierce nativism of the 1920s and the grim and frustrating Great Depression of the 1930s kept them pretty much in the poverty of the immigrant neighborhoods. Only a few managed to claw their way out into middle-class respectability. But in the three decades since the end of the Second World War, an extraordinary economic and social phenomenon has occurred: The ethnics have made it. The Italians are now the third richest religio-ethnic group in American society—second only to Jews and Irish Catholics—and the Poles earn almost $1,000 a year more than the average white American in metropolitan areas of the North. In the middle 1940s, the curve of college attendance for young people for both Italians and Poles began to swing upward, so that by the 1960s, Poles and Italians of college age were *more* likely to attend college than the national average for white Americans.

Without anyone's noticing it, those who were doomed to be failures by their race, religion, language, and family backgrounds have now succeeded. Few of them are wealthy, some are still poor; but on the average their incomes are substantially higher than those of other white Americans living in the same cities and regions of the United States. Many Americans reject in principle the possibility of such a miracle; some of the ethnic leaders themselves (in a perhaps unintentional ethnic joke) vigorously deny the success of their own people; yet the data are beyond any reasonable doubt. In a very short space of time, the length of one generation, more or less, the American dream has come true; and some of the people who were children in the Stanislowowo in 1920 have lived to see and to enjoy the achievement of their dream. Even the Stanislowowo has changed for those who remain. The well fed, neatly dressed, scrupulously clean children who troop out of St. Stanislaus Kostka on a spring afternoon—grandchildren, perhaps, of the women who worked sixty hours a week in sweatshops filled with the stench of manure—are clearly the offspring of an affluent society. . . .

However patriarchal the family structures may have been, the women of the ethnic immigrants went to work from the beginning—long before it became an upper-middle-class fashion. The income of many wage earners in a family no doubt provided an economic base for the ethnics to make

their initial breakthrough—which occurred, perhaps, some-
time in the early 1950s. (Data on neighborhood concentra-
tion of various ethnic communities indicate that the Poles
finally began to move out from the center of the city at that
time.) But by 1970, the women in Polish and Italian families
were no more likely to have jobs than their nonethnic coun-
terparts in the large cities of the North. So the income
achievement of the southern and eastern European Catholics
cannot be explained by multiple-wage earners in the family
—though there is a possibility that many of the men and
some of the women may also have second and third jobs.
Nor do the 25 years of prosperity between 1945 and 1970
explain the "ethnic miracle," though they obviously created
an environment in which such a miracle could occur. For
not only did the ethnics improve their income during that
quarter century, as did virtually everyone else, but they improved it *disproportionately*. At the end of the quarter century, not only were they better off than in 1945, they had
improved their relative position in comparison with the rest
of the population. Prosperity, in other words, provided the
opportunity for the "ethnic miracle," but the miracle itself
was a response to the opportunity. . . .

The Legacy of the Immigrants

So one must still face the puzzle: Despite the virtually
unanimous opinion of educated Americans a half century
ago, the children and the grandchildren of eastern and
southern European immigrants have achieved not only economic equality but economic superiority, on the average, in
the United States. They were not supposed to be able to do
it; to many people it is incredible that they have done it;
and to almost everyone the explanation of their success is
obscure. Now we see that the ethnics in the quarter century
between the end of the Second World War and the end of
the Vietnamese War did exactly what the Jews had done in
the previous quarter century—and with apparent ease.

How did they manage it? The immigrants themselves
were ambitious. Perhaps they were the enterprising and
courageous young people in their own societies—and young

they were. When we see movies like *Hester Street,* many of us are astonished to discover that the immigrants from eastern and southern Europe were disproportionately young, and either unmarried or just recently married. We all have a recollection of an old grandparent whom we knew during childhood, and without giving the matter much thought, we tend to imagine the immigrants themselves as old—forgetting that the old *babushka* or *mamacita* was once as young as we were.

The immigrants came from a Europe which, as one American historian has remarked, "invited desertion." The population expansion of the middle nineteenth century had created a land-hungry peasant class for whom there was no room either on the farms or in the cities. They came to the United States seeking the "good life," the kind of life that owning land made possible. They were fully prepared to work hard; indeed, a life of anything but hard work was beyond their comprehension. They would work hard to make money. . . . Desperately poor people themselves, with scores of generations of poverty behind them, the immigrants could imagine no other way to live besides scrimping, sacrificing, saving. America did them no favors, gave them no special treatment, in fact discriminated against them, forced them into the most menial occupations and the most miserable housing, and exploited them through the most corrupt political structures in the country. Americans hated them, despised them, condemned them, and eventually tried to bar their relatives from joining them; they joked about them, stereotyped them, and tried to change them into "good Americans" by making them ashamed of their own heritages.

The Poles and the Italians, like the Irish and the Jews before them, bitterly resented such treatment, but they did not grow angry at the United States, for even though it did them no favors, it still provided them with two things they would never have had in the old country: personal freedom and the opportunity to convert the hard work they took for granted into economic progress. In the old country, hard work got you nothing; in the United States it got you, or at least your children or their children, a chance.

Hard work, saving, sacrifice—such is a tentative explanation of the "ethnic miracle." Ironically, the Catholic ethnics turned out to be very good at these "Protestant" and "American" traits that the Dillingham Commission thought they could never learn. To work hard, to save, to be ambitious for oneself and one's children—the immigrants needed no "Americanization" to learn that way of life. They came here with a dream; it was not that they expected something for nothing, but rather that their hard work would earn them something. For some of them, for many of their children, and for most of their grandchildren the dream came true. [The anti-immigrant Dillingham Commission of the early 1900s, chaired by Senator William Paul Dillingham of Vermont, favored the quota system set up in 1921 by the Senator's bill.—Ed.]

Is that how it happened? It would seem so, though until much more careful study of the history of immigrant families is done, we will not know for sure. And it should be done in the relatively near future, while some of the immigrants and their oldest children are still alive to be interviewed. But curiously enough, many Americans, including ethnics like Michael Novak, are much more eager to believe that the American dream has not come true for the ethnics. If it hasn't, then there is nothing to explain.

In the process of economic achievement, have the ethnics "assimilated"? Have they absorbed the values and beliefs and behavior patterns of the host culture? To begin with, they came with many values in common. They were, after all, products of the same white-European, Judaeo-Christian heritage. They learned to speak English quickly, they wore the same clothes, listened to the same radio and television programs, read the same newspapers; and yet a remarkable diversity of values, attitudes, styles, opinions, and behavior has persisted. Affection and authority, for example, are recognizably different in Jewish, Italian, Polish, and Irish families, as are the styles with which they approach politics, the ways in which they consume alcohol, and the ultimate views they hold about human nature and the nature of the universe.

Ethnicity and American Culture

Furthermore, these differences do not seem to diminish with the number of generations ethnics have been in the United States or with the amount of education they have had. In a loose, pluralistic society like the United States, economic success and rather harmonious adjustment to other groups can be achieved while still maintaining a partially distinctive culture. Indeed, such a distinctive culture can be maintained without having to be self-conscious about it. The Irish propensity for politics and alcohol, for example, and the Polish propensity to vote (Poles have the highest voting rates of any American religio-ethnic group) are not affected by ethnic self-consciousness or militancy. The anxiety of the Dillingham Commission and its nativist successors about whether diversity threatened America's "common culture" missed the whole point: In America the common culture validates diversity in theory, if not in practice. You can be anything you want—religiously, culturally, stylistically—so long as you are committed to the fundamental political principles of the republic.

Ethnicity is not a way of looking back to the old world. Most of the immigrants were only too happy to get the hell out of it. Ethnicity is rather a way of being American, a way of defining yourself into the pluralistic culture which existed before you arrived. The last thing in the world the new ethnic upper-middle class wants is to define themselves out of the common American culture. Why should they? America may have done them no favors, but it still has been better to them than any society their families ever knew.

So the militant ethnic somewhere out there in "middle America"—hard hat on his head and gun in his hand, ready to tear society apart by resisting the advances of the non-white immigrants—is almost entirely a fiction of the imagination of liberals and leftists in the media and the academy. The ethnic may not always like some of the things he sees and hears on television, but his standard of living has doubled at least in the last quarter century, so he is not angry at the "American way"; he is not about to do anything to endanger his still precarious respectability and affluence. He may rejoice that the black activism of the 1960s has legitimated his somewhat more explicit and conscious pride in heritage, but the "ethnic revival" or the "new ethnic militancy" is largely another fiction of the liberal imagination.

Nor has the ethnic turned to the right. He is neither a "rugged individualist" nor a political reactionary, as many left-liberal commentators would so dearly like to believe. On social legislation, the Italian, Polish, and for that matter, Irish Catholics are still left of center, still members of the New Deal coalition. They did not disproportionately defect from the Democratic party to vote against George McGovern, nor were they strong supporters of George Wallace in the 1968 presidential election. The myth of the massive Polish vote for Wallace is so powerful that it is practically impossible to debunk; yet the Poles were the most likely of all gentile groups to vote for Hubert Humphrey, and substantially less than the 6 percent non-Southern vote for Wallace was recorded among Polish Catholics. It would surely be inaccurate to think of the children, grandchildren, and great grandchildren of the ethnics as left-wing liberals or militant integrationists (most militants seem to live in the suburbs), but on virtually every political and social issue facing the country today, the ethnics are either at the center or to the left of it. Their Irish coreligionists are either close to or just behind the Jews on most measures of liberalism. I do not expect such data to be believed, because too many people have too much emotional energy invested in the opposite opinion. The data, nevertheless, are impossible to ignore.

So the "ethnic miracle" was accomplished without the complete loss of values or family structures—and without a right-wing backlash either. Indeed it was accomplished without any notable desertion from the Democratic party. The Stanislowowians and their children and grandchildren apparently made it despite their Polish values and family structure.

But is the word "despite" appropriate? Might there be a possibility that there was something in the culture of the immigrants that actually facilitated the "ethnic miracle"? Preliminary but sophisticated research conducted both at the Department of Labor and the National Bureau of Economic Research (NBER) suggests that Catholics and Jews are more successful in American society than Protestants because of some special factor at work in their early childhood —perhaps a closer and more intense attention from parents. As Thomas Juster of the NBER observes:

Economists and other social scientists have recently begun to pay close attention to the possible role of preschool investments in children by parents as it affects subsequent educational attainment . . . [and to the] possible influence on earnings of different amounts of parental time spent with preschool or school-age children. . . . Taking account of family background factors like father's and mother's education and occupation, variables for both Jewish and Catholic religious preference have a significant (positive) impact on reported earnings relative to respondents' reporting of Protestant preference. . . . Plausible hypotheses are that they reflect differences in the cultural background to which the respondents were exposed during formative years or differences in the quality or quantity of parental time inputs. . . .

Not only the Dillingham Commission but even the Protestant ethic has been stood on its head; the familial culture of the ethnics, their stubborn differences in family values, may well have turned out to be an economic asset. In the absence of further research, such a possibility will remain an intriguing speculation. (Let it be noted again that while ambition, hard work, and strong family support for achievement may have been the path to upward mobility for the white ethnics, it does not follow that the same path can or must be followed by more recent immigrants. The ethnic miracle is worth studying in itself even if it has no pertinence to more recent social problems or provides only useful insights for considering those problems.) . . .

Recovering the Past

If there is any ethnic militancy at all, it is to be found not in the vast middle and lower reaches of income and occupational prestige but rather among the elite, those college-educated and graduate-school-educated ethnics who bump up against the residual nativism still present in the upper strata of American society. It is not the Slovakian steelworkers but the Michael Novaks who are the most likely to be angry—and with good reason. Or, as far as that goes, it is not the Irish cop or the Irish politician or the Irish attorney who grows angry at elite nativism, for they either do not encounter it or it does not affect them. (The reader may judge for himself whether the author of this article is an angry militant.)

Those of us who stand on the shoulders of the immigrants are ill at ease with our predecessors. Their raw acquisitiveness embarrasses us, and their sacrifices and sufferings cause us pain. It is hard to admit that we owe a great deal to those who came before us. We repress memories of places like the Stanislowowo in the same way we repress memories of such disasters as the Spanish Influenza or the Great Depression; they are too terrible and too close for us to think about very much. It took a long, long time before a movie like *Hester Street* could be made, and it may be another generation or two before the descendants of those brave, strong, ambitious young people who swarmed into this country between 1890 and 1914 will be able to relax sufficiently to place those urban pioneers alongside the other brave people who came over the Appalachian mountains a century earlier to pioneer an unexplored continent. The miracle of the frontier is now a standard part of American mythology. Perhaps by the tricentennial the ethnic miracle will have become one of the respected marvels of the American story.

BILINGUAL EDUCATION [5]

Arguments For and Against Bilingual Education

Opponents of bilingual education charge that it weakens the common American glue and aggravates ethnic tensions and differences. "It happens to be terribly fashionable right now to proclaim that the whole ideal of a common Amer-

[5] Excerpts from report by Sandra Stencel, staff writer. *Editorial Research Reports.* v 2, no 7:622–4, 626–8. Ag. 19, '77. Reprinted by permission.

ican nation was a brutally oppressive delusion," declared Professor Stephen Thernstrom, a Harvard social historian. "But though the old pressure to Americanize immigrants was pretty heavy-handed at times, essentially I think it was necessary. It's not possible to operate in a complex society with twenty different languages. . . ."

Similar views have been expressed by Harvard sociologist Nathan Glazer. "I believe the 'Americanization' of the immigrant was a great achievement, an almost unique and unparalleled achievement despite its harshness and arrogance," Glazer wrote in 1974. "I am not sure that the immigrants who came to this country willingly, to work and to become citizens of a new land, were deprived when they gave up an old language for English, old cultures for a new emerging culture, old allegiances for new allegiances."

Some educators see bilingual programs as a push for jobs and power rather than an educational vehicle to help children. . . .

Stephen S. Rosenfeld, in a widely circulated and often-quoted column that originally appeared in the Washington *Post* on September 22, 1974, expressed the fear that bilingual education "might make kids even less competent and less motivated to deal in a competitive English-speaking society." Some parents and educators also are worried about the expense of bilingual education at a time when schools are having to cut back on music, art, athletics and other special programs.

Supporters of bilingual education dismiss these claims as exaggerated. "The concept of bilingualism is greatly misunderstood," declared Don Wong, director of the Chinese American Heritage Projects of the San Francisco Association of Chinese teachers. "It's not an attempt to compete with the English language. It's a bridge for language minorities to gain equal access and participation in American society." Answering charges that bilingual education aggravates ethnic tensions, Herbert Teitelbaum, legal director of the Puerto Rican Legal Defense and Education Fund, wrote: "Ethnic tensions are created not by bilingual education but, on the contrary, by notions of language and cultural superiority that have formed a basis for much of the resistance to bilingual education."

Advocates of bilingual instruction say it offers the fastest way of cutting down the language barriers which for years doomed millions of American pupils to academic retardation or failure. "A child who starts off with frustration or failure may never catch up," wrote Muriel R. Saville and Rudolph C. Troike of the Center for Applied Linguistics. (Muriel R. Saville and Rudolph C. Troike, *A Handbook of Bilingual Education*, revised edition, 1971, p. 2. The Center for Applied Linguistics, established in 1959, is an independent, nonprofit, professional organization which serves as a national research, development and information center in language and linguistics.)

The best argument for bilingual education, its supporters say, is the discouraging academic performance of youngsters with English-language difficulties. The educational handicaps of Hispanic children were outlined in a report issued May 20, 1977, by the National Assessment of Educational Progress funded by and under contract with the National Center for Education Statistics. Hispanic children tested consistently below the national average in reading, science, mathematics, social studies and career development and repeated more grades than other children. . . .

Equally dismal statistics are recorded for American Indians. Dropout rates for Indian children are twice the national average. Indian achievement levels are two or three years below white achievement levels and decline the longer an Indian child stays in school. Only about one third of the Indian people have finished high school. . . .

Dual Language Instruction in Early America

"America is God's Crucible, the great Melting Pot where all the races of Europe are melting and re-forming." In those words playwright Israel Zangwill, a British-born Jew, described his vision of America—a country where diverse ethnic and religious groups soon blended into a homogeneous mass. The myth of the "melting pot" had a prominent place in American thought even before Zangwill coined the phrase in 1908. French-American author Michel Guillaume Jean de Crèvecœur, in his *Letters from an American Farmer,* wrote in 1782 that in the United States "individuals of all nations are melted into a new race of men."

Despite the prevalence and popularity of the melting pot myth, instances of non-English and bilingual education were not uncommon in eighteenth and nineteenth century America. Before the Civil War, German-English public schools existed in several states. There also were French-English programs in Louisiana and Spanish-English programs in the Territory of New Mexico. Norwegian, Czech, Italian, Polish and Dutch also were occasionally taught in American public schools during this period. In addition, bilingual instruction flourished in many private (chiefly church) schools set up for immigrant children from eastern and southern Europe.

A few states enacted legislation permitting the use of a language other than English as a medium of instruction. For example, Pennsylvania passed a law in 1837 and Ohio in 1839 authorizing German-English public schools. New Mexico in 1884 allowed each school district to decide whether instruction would be in Spanish, English or both. Throughout the 1800s the Cherokee Indian nation provided bilingual education for its people. The Cherokees developed an educational system of more than two hundred schools and academies, which, according to Arnold H. Leibowitz, produced a "population 90 per cent literate in its native language and used bilingual materials to such an extent that Oklahoma Cherokees had a higher English literacy level than the white populations of either Texas or Arkansas."

Nationalism, Xenophobia, and Public Schools

Many bilingual and foreign-language schools disappeared in the wave of nationalism, anti-Catholicism and xenophobia that swept the United States in the late 1800s and early 1900s. Most educators who advocated English-only instruction believed in the melting pot theory. Ellwood P. Cubberly, a well-known educational historian of that era, characterized new immigrants to the United States as "illiterate, docile, lacking in self-reliance and initiative, and not possessing the Anglo-Teutonic conceptions of law, order and government." The role of the schools, in Cubberly's view, was "to assimilate and amalgamate these people as part of the American race. . . ."

This assimilationist position was sanctioned at the highest levels of government. Theodore Roosevelt, in his book *The Foes of Our Household* (1917), wrote that "any man who comes here . . . must adopt the institutions of the United States, and therefore he must adopt the language which is now the native tongue of our people. . . . It would be not merely a misfortune but a crime to perpetuate differences of language in this country."

Even then some Americans did not accept the melting pot philosophy. In an influential series of articles in *The Nation* magazine in 1915, Horace M. Kallan argued that American culture had much to gain by permitting each immigrant group to develop its own particular tendencies. Advocates of cultural pluralism continued to speak out during the following decades, but it was not until the early 1960s that public bilingual schooling was reborn.

CULTURAL PLURALISM AND THE SCHOOLS [6]

During the Colonial period, many different ethnic and nationality groups immigrated to North America to practice freely their religious and political beliefs and to improve their economic status. These groups were provincial, ethnocentric, and intolerant of ethnic differences. Each nationality group tried desperately to establish European institutions on American soil and to remake North America in the image of its native land.

Very early in Colonial history the English became the dominant ethnic group, and controlled entry to most social,

[6] Article by James A. Banks, professor of education; Spencer Fellow, Social Studies and Ethnic Studies, University of Washington. *Education Digest.* 40:21–3. Ap. '75. This article is condensed from the original which was published in *Educational Leadership.* 32:163–6. D. '74. Reprinted by permission.

economic, and political institutions. The English did not allow immigrants from other nations to participate fully in the social system. Thus, the attainment of Anglo characteristics became a requisite for full societal participation. Immigrants who remained distinctly "ethnic" were punished and ridiculed.

The public schools, like other social institutions, were dominated by Anglo-Americans. One of their major functions was to rid children of ethnic characteristics and to make them culturally Anglo-Saxon. The schools taught the children of immigrants contempt for their cultures and forced them to experience self-alienation and self-rejection. The melting-pot ideology became the philosophical justification for the cultural and ethnic destruction which the schools promoted. All European cultures, it was argued, were to be blended and from them a novel and superior culture would emerge. Most immigrants, however, abandoned their cultures and attained Anglo cultural characteristics. One dominant culture emerged rather than a synthesis of diverse cultures.

In many significant ways, the Anglo-dominated society, and the schools which helped to perpetuate it, succeeded both in acculturating European-Americans and in helping them to attain inclusion into mainstream American life. Today most American children of European descent find the school culture highly consistent with their culture, although a few do not.

Many ethnic minority youths find the school culture alien, hostile, and self-defeating. Because of institutional racism, poverty, and other complex factors, most ethnic minority communities are characterized by numerous values, institutions, behavior patterns, and linguistic traits which differ in significant ways from the dominant society. The youths who are socialized within these ethnic communities enter the school with cultural characteristics which the school rejects and demeans. Because of the negative ways in which their cultural and racial traits are viewed by the school, educators fail to help most minority youths to acquire the skills which they need to function effectively within the two cultural worlds in which they must survive. Consequently, many of them drop out of school, psychologically and physically.

Role of Multicultural School

What should be the role of the school within a democratic society which has a dominant culture and many other cultures? The school in this type of society has a difficult task, especially when those who make most of the major public decisions do not value, and often disdain, the minority cultures. Although cultural pluralism exists within American society, most major decisions in government and in industry are made by Anglo-Americans, many of whom are ethnocentric and intolerant of cultural, ethnic, and racial differences.

The school must help Anglo-Americans to break out of their ethnic encapsulations and to learn that there are other viable cultures in the United States, aspects of which can help to redeem and to revivify the dominant culture. The school should also help all students to develop *ethnic literacy*, since most Americans are very ignorant about cultures other than their own. To attain social and economic mobility, minorities are required to function in the dominant culture and are thus forced out of their ethnic encapsulations. Most minorities, nevertheless, are very ignorant about other minorities.

Broadly conceptualized ethnic heritage programs should be devised and implemented in all schools. Such programs should teach about the experiences of *all* American ethnic groups. Most ethnic studies programs now in the schools deal only with the history and culture of the ethnic minority group which is present or dominant within the local school population.

Thus, it is rare to find an ethnic heritage program within a predominantly black school which teaches about the experiences of Asian-Americans, Mexican-Americans, and Puerto Rican–Americans. Such narrowly conceptualized ethnic studies programs do not help students develop the global view of ethnicity in the United States which they need to become effective change agents. We have reached a point in our history in which multiethnic approaches to the teaching of ethnic studies are not only appropriate but essential.

The school within a pluralistic society should maximize the cultural and economic options of students from all income and ethnic groups. Minority students should be helped to attain the skills needed to function effectively both within their ethnic cultures and within the dominant culture.

By arguing that the school must help minority youths to attain the skills needed to function effectively within the dominant culture, I do not mean to suggest that the school should continue to demean the languages and cultures of minority students. Rather, educators should respect the cultural and linguistic characteristics of minority youths, and change the curriculum so that it will reflect their learning and cultural styles and greatly enhance their achievement. Minority students should not be taught contempt for their cultures. Teachers should use elements of their cultures to help them to attain the skills needed to live alternative life styles.

Cultural Options

Anglo-American students should also be taught that they have cultural options. They should realize that using black English is one effective way to communicate, that Native Americans have values, beliefs, and lifestyles which may be functional for them, and that there are alternative ways of behaving and of viewing the universe which are practiced within the United States that they can freely embrace. By helping Anglo-American students to view the world beyond their cultural perspectives, we will enrich them as human beings and enable them to live more productive and fulfilling lives.

It is necessary but not sufficient for the school to help minority children to acquire the skills which they need to attain economic and social mobility. It must also help equip them with the skills, attitudes, and abilities needed to attain *power* so that they can effectively participate in the reformation of the social system.

While the school should reflect and perpetuate cultural diversity, it has a responsibility to teach a commitment to and respect for the core values expressed in our major historical documents. If carried to the extreme, cultural pluralism can be used to justify racism, cultural genocide, and related practices. Thus, this concept must be rigorously examined for all of its social and philosophical ramifications.

We should not exaggerate the extent of cultural pluralism in the United States, and should realize that widespread cultural assimilation has taken place in America. To try to perceive cultural differences where none exist may be as detrimental as ignoring those which are real. The school should foster those cultural differences which maximize opportunities for democratic living but vigorously oppose those which do not. Emerging concepts and unexamined ideas must not be used to divert attention from the humanistic goals that we have too long deferred, or from the major cause of our social ills—*institutional racism*.

THE LIMITS OF ETHNICITY [7]

Americans have often defined themselves through an unwillingness to define themselves. In the work of our greatest writers, notably Melville and Whitman, the refusal to succumb to fixity of definition comes to seem a cultural signature.

In opposition there has arisen a native industry of American-definers who offer a maddening plenitude of answers. But people in a hurry with answers have usually not even heard the questions. And finally it all comes to the same thing: many answers equal no answer.

All through the nineteenth century there was a lot of talk in America about our national character, our unique emerging culture, our new kind of man. Most of it was no more than talk. But the real cultures of America were meanwhile being built up as *regional* cultures, defining them-

[7] An article by Irving Howe, author, historian, critic. *New Republic*. 176:17–19. Je. 25, '77. Reprinted by permission of *The New Republic*. Copyright © 1977 The New Republic, Inc.

selves apart from and sometimes in opposition to the idea of
a single national culture. Our best writers, enraptured with
particularities of speech and place, felt that in local custom
they might find an essence of the new nation.

With time, the regions came to be replaced by immigrant communities. The heterogeneity of nineteenth century America, consisting of regions often at considerable
physical and spiritual distance from one another, was followed by the heterogeneity of industrial America, consisting of immigrant subcultures, plebeian and urban, which
clung to some indeterminate condition between the remem-
bered Old Country and the not-so-friendly New World.

The most recent sign of Amercian heterogeneity has
been a turn toward ethnicity. In part, this is mere fashion
concocted by TV, publicity and other agencies of deceit. In
part, it releases deep impulses of yearning. No one quite
knows what ethnicity means: that is why it's so useful a
term. For if we will not define ourselves as Americans, we
can at least define ourself as fractional or hyphenated Americans, making of that hardy hyphen a kind of seesaw of
cultural ambivalence. Or we will define ourselves as pre-
Americans, claiming recognition for what can barely still
be recognized in us—the heritage of European nationhood
and culture.

There are plenty of symptoms. There is my own recent
book about immigrant Jews [*World of Our Fathers,* 1976],
written, I must plead, in innocence of the uses to which it
may be put. There is another recent book about the ordeal
of black slaves and the journey that one of their descendants
made back home. No doubt there will be many more books
on such themes, some of them serious and others devoted to
making a quick buck.

It is all astonishing. In a country long devoted to dulling
the sense of the historical past and denying the continuity
of experience from Europe to America; in a country where
the young can hardly remember the name of Franklin Del-
ano Roosevelt and are by no means sure in which century
World War I was fought, or who fought in it—in this very
country groups of people now seek to define themselves

through a deliberate exclusion from the dominant native stock which, only yesterday, had been taking pains to exclude them. These ethnic groups now turn back—and as they nervously insist, "with pride"—to look for fragments of a racial or national or religious identity that moves them to the extent that it is no longer available. Perhaps, also, *because* it is no longer available.

Some of this turning-back strikes me as a last hurrah of nostalgia. Each day, necessarily, it keeps getting weaker and sillier. Traveling around the country recently, I encountered middle-class Jewish ladies intent on discovering their family genealogies. I suggested to them, not very graciously, that if they were serious they would first try to learn their people's history and then they might see that it hardly mattered whether they came from the Goldbergs of eastern Poland or the Goldbergs of the western Ukraine. Other segments of the Jewish community are turning back to the immigrant experience. Some time ago I attended a pageant in an eastern city recreating the Lower East Side: pushcarts, onion rolls, flexibly-priced suits, etc. Someone asked me whether anything was missing and I answered, again not very graciously, that a touch of reality might have been added by a tubercular garment worker spitting blood from his years of exhaustion in a sweat shop.

Sentimentalism is the besetting sin of the Jewish turn to ethnicity, a sentimentalism that would erase memories of ugliness and pathology, disputation and radicalism. Among the blacks things are different. Having been deprived of their history in more brutal ways than anyone else in our society, they have to engage in more extreme measures to retrieve it. Still, one wonders whether some recent assertions of roots are a conquest of history or an improvisation of myth. Tens of thousands of black Americans are expected to be visiting Gambia this summer, and while that is likely to be a boon for the tourist industry of a country that needs every break it can get, one is less certain about what it will do for the tourists. Will it lead to a growing moral strength with which to confront American realities or will it constitute a pleasant style of evasion?

Still, I would be the last to deny that there are serious
meanings behind ethnic nostalgia. We are all aware that
our ties with the European past grow increasingly feeble.
Yet we feel uneasy before the prospect of becoming "just
Americans." We feel uneasy before the prospect of becoming
as indistinguishable from one another as our motel rooms
are, or as flavorless and mass-produced as the bread many
of us eat.

We are losing the passions, the words, the customs of the
old countries. Having savored the richness of bilingualism,
we find it distressing to be reduced to one language—at most.
And so we reach back, clumsily, to a past we know cannot
be regained.

To the grandeur of the American idea we want to con-
nect the historical substance of the Jewish or black or Slavic
experience. All of these subcultures add a little flavor to
modern American life, which certainly can use it. Walk into
Little Italy and you feel an enclosingness of human bonds
that you're not likely to feel in many other parts of New
York City. Watch the Greek-Americans parade on Fifth
Avenue, with their garish floats evoking symbols not many
of the paraders could identify, and you feel, well, let them
cling to as much of their past as they can. And as for black
culture as an avenue for difference in America—one that
brings us into greater sadness and suffering than Americans
can usually confront—that has by now become a virtual
cliche of our culture and thereby properly subject to skep-
ticism by blacks themselves.

The famous melting-pot of American society could grow
very hot, indeed, too hot for those being melted. Usually it
was the immigrants and their children who were the meltees,
while the temperature was being regulated by the WASP
melters. So by now many of us are rightly suspicious about
easy notions concerning cultural assimilation, what might
be called the bleaching of America. Some of us remember
with discomfort our days in high school when well-inten-
tioned but willful teachers tried to smooth the Jewish
creases out of our speech and our psyches. We don't want
to be smoothed out—at least entirely, at least not yet. We

don't want to yield ourselves completely to that "destruction of memories" which the great sociologist, W. I. Thomas, once said was the essence of the Americanizing process.

Neither should we succumb to the current uncritical glorification of ethnicity. The ethnic impulse necessarily carries with it dangers of parochialism: the smugness of snug streets as against the perilous visions of large cities, the indulgent celebration of habitual ways simply because they are habitual. The ethnic community always runs the danger that it is not really preserving the riches of an old-world culture; it is merely clinging to some scraps and debris of that culture which were brought across the ocean. At a time when the fate of mankind is increasingly, for better or worse, an *international* fate, the ethnic community too often shuts its eyes or buries its head while clinging anxiously to received customs—as if there were no more important things in the world than customs!

When one thinks a little about the culture of our time, the force of these cautions regarding ethnicity is magnified. At its best and most troubling modernist expression, the culture of the twentieth century has broken past borders of nationhood, race and speech. There is a characteristic pattern here: province runs smack against metropolis, decaying tradition jostles metropolitan experiment—and the result is that brilliant nervousness, that fierce and restless probing we identify with modernist culture. Cavafy from the streets of Alexandria, Faulkner from the hills and villages of Mississippi, Sholom Aleichem from the east European *shtetl* [small town or village], Eliot from a provincial midwestern city, Joyce from the rigid precincts of Dublin—our greatest twentieth century writers leave behind them, though finally they remain deeply stamped by, the limitations of the provincial. The province, the ethnic nest, remains the point from which everything begins and without which, probably, it could not begin; but the province, the ethnic nest, is not enough, it must be transcended.

Finally, however, the great weakness of the turn to ethnicity is that it misreads or ignores the realities of power in

America. The central problems of our society have to do, not with ethnic groupings, but with economic policy, social rule, class relations. They have to do with vast inequities of wealth, with the shameful neglect of a growing class of subproletarians, with the readiness of policy makers to tolerate high levels of unemployment. They have to do with "the crisis of the cities," a polite phrase masking a terrible reality—the willingness of this country to dump millions of black (and white) poor into the decaying shells of once thriving cities.

Toward problems of this kind and magnitude, what answers can ethnicity offer? Very weak ones, I fear. Common action by the poor, major movements for social change require alignments that move past ethnic divisions. They require a tougher perception of the nature of American society than the ethnic impulse usually enables. The dominant powers of American society would be perfectly delighted if, for example, American blacks were to divert themselves over the next ten or twenty years in seeking their roots in distant Africa, especially if this meant that blacks would thereby lessen their pressure for the jobs, the housing, the opportunities they need here. (Who can say with any assurance that the vivid, if coarse, evocation of the black ordeal in the recent TV version of *Roots* did very much, or anything at all, to persuade white Americans that this society owes a debt to its black minority? Who can say that it raised the consciousness of TV viewers regarding current social policy rather than giving them a momentary *frisson*, an inexpensive thrill of horror?) Social militancy may not always be undermined, social solidarity may not always be threatened, by ethnic or racial consciousness; but too often in the past, they have been.

In principle, is there any reason why discovering that "black is beautiful" shouldn't lead to the conclusion, "well, if we're beautiful, or even if we're not, we deserve a bigger share of the pie than America has thus far let us get"? No, of course not—in principle. Nor is there any preordained reason why the white ethnic groups could not move from a reconquest of identity to union with other plebeian communities in behalf of shared needs, thereby helping a little to right the wrongs of our society.

This is not just a problem in social strategy; it has also to do with human awareness and self-definition. We want to remain, for the little time that we can, whatever it was that we were before they started pressurizing us in those melting pots. So let's try, even if the historical odds are against us. But there is also another moral possibility, one that we call in Yiddish being or becoming a *mensch*. The word suggests a vision of humanity or humaneness; it serves as a norm, a possibility beckoning us. You don't have to be Jewish (or non-Jewish), you don't have to be white (or black) in order to be a *mensch*. Keeping one eye upon the fading past and the other on the unclear future, enlarging ethnic into ethic, you can become a man or woman of the world, even as you remember, perhaps because you remember, the tongue your grandfather and grandmother spoke in, though in fact the words themselves are fading from memory.

BIBLIOGRAPHY

An asterisk (*) preceding a reference indicates that the article or part of it has been reprinted in this book.

BOOKS

Armstrong, V. I. comp. I have spoken; American history through the voices of the Indians. Swallow Press. '71.

Aswad, B. C. comp. Arabic speaking communities in American cities. Ozer. '74.
Published by Center for Migration Studies of New York and Association of Arab-American University Graduates.

*Bahr, H. M. and others, eds. Native Americans today: sociological perspectives. Harper & Row. '71.
Reprinted in this issue: Report on legal services to the Indians: a study in desperation. L. K. Halverson. p 338–44.

Baldwin, G. C. The Apache Indians. Four Winds Press. '78.

Berthoff, R. T. British immigrants in industrial America, 1790-1950. Harvard University Press. '53; Russell & Russell. '68.

Blegen, T. C. ed. Land of their choice; the immigrants write home. University of Minnesota Press. '55.

Buenker, J. D. and Burckel, N. C. eds. Immigration and ethnicity: a guide to information sources. (American Government and History Information Guide Series) Gale. '78.

Bundy, Robert, ed. Images of the future; the 21st century and beyond. Prometheus Books. '76.

Burnette, Robert. The tortured Americans. Prentice-Hall. '71.

Cafferty, P. S. J. and Chestang, Leon, eds. The diverse society. National Association of Social Workers. 1425 H St. N.W. Washington, DC 20005. '76.
See especially: Ethnicity and health delivery systems. Leona Grossman. p 129–48.

Cordasco, Francesco, ed. Studies in Italian American social history; essays in honor of Leonard Covello. Rowman & Littlefield. '75.

Cortés, C. E. and others. Three perspectives on ethnicity—blacks, Chicanos, and native Americans. Capricorn/Putnam. '76.

*Du Bois, W. E. B. The souls of black folk. Fawcett. '61.
Originally published 1903.

*Elazar, Daniel and Friedman Murray. Moving up: ethnic succession in America. Institute on Pluralism and Group Identity. 165 E. 56th St. New York, NY 10022. '76.

Farb, Peter. Man's rise to civilization as shown by the Indians of North America from primeval times to the coming of the industrial state. Dutton. '68.

Feinstein, Otto, ed. Ethnic groups in the city; culture, institutions, and power. Heath Lexington Books. '71.

Fellows, D. K. A mosaic of America's ethnic minorities. John Wiley & Sons. '72.

Fey, H. E. and McNickle, D'Arcy. Indians and other Americans; two ways of life meet. Harper. '59.

Fitzpatrick, J. P. Puerto Rican Americans; the meaning of migration to the mainland. Prentice-Hall. '71.

Forbes, J. D. ed. The Indian in America's past. Prentice-Hall. '64.

Frazier, E. F. The Negro family in the United States. rev. and abr. ed. University of Chicago. '66.
    Original edition. University of Chicago. 1939.

Fuchs, L. H. ed. American ethnic politics. Harper & Row. '68.

Furer, H. B. ed. The British in America, 1578-1970; a chronology and fact book. (Ethnic Chronology Series, no7) Oceana Publications. '72.

*Garcia, R. A. comp. & ed. The Chicanos in America, 1540-1974; a chronology & fact book. (Ethnic Chronology Series, no26) Oceana Publications. '77.
    Reprinted in this issue: Significance of the Mexican-American people. J. D. Forbes. p 25–34.

*Glazer, Nathan and Moynihan, D. P. Beyond the melting pot. MIT and Harvard University. '63.
    A second, revised edition was published by MIT Press in 1970.

Glazer, Nathan and others, eds. Ethnicity; theory and experience. Harvard University Press. '75.
    Product of a conference held at the American Academy of Arts and Sciences, Brookline, Massachusetts in October 1972.

Goldston, R. C. The Negro revolution. Macmillan. '68.

*Greeley, A. M. Why can't they be like us? America's white ethnic groups. Institute of Human Relations Press. '69.
    Revised and enlarged edition published by Dutton in 1971.

Green, A. W. Sociology. McGraw-Hill. '64.

Greenspan, C. L. and Hirsch, L. M. comps. All those voices: the minority experience. Macmillan. '71.

Gross, T. L. ed. A nation of nations; ethnic literature in America. Free Press. '71.

Gutman, H. G. The black family in slavery and freedom, 1750-1925. Vintage Books. '77.

Hagopian, E. C. and Paden, Ann, eds. The Arab Americans: studies in assimilation. Medina University Press International. Wilmette, IL 60091. '69.

Haley, Alex. Roots: the saga of an American family. Doubleday. '76.
    Review. Time. 108:109. O. 18, '76. R. Z. Sheppard.

Handlin, Oscar. The uprooted. 2d enl. ed. Little, Brown. '73.

Hansen, M. L. The Atlantic migration, 1607-1860; a history of the continuing settlement of the United States. Harvard University Press. '45.

*Highwater, Jamake. Indian America. (Fodor's Modern Guides) McKay. '75.

*Hill, Herbert, ed. Anger, and beyond; the Negro writer in the U.S. Harper & Row. '66.
    Reprinted in this book: Philistinism and the Negro writer. LeRoi Jones (Amiri Baraka). p 51–61.

Hosokawa, Bill. Nisei; the quiet Americans. Morrow. '69.

Howard, J. R. ed. Awakening minorities: American Indians, Mexican Americans, Puerto Ricans. Aldine. '70.

Josephy, A. M. The Indian heritage of America. Knopf. '68.

Kallen, H. M. Cultural pluralism and the American idea. University of Pennsylvania. '56.

Kennedy, J. F. A nation of immigrants. rev. & enl. ed. H. Hamilton. '64.

King, Florence. Wasp, where is thy sting? Stein & Day. '77.

Kitano, H. H. L. Japanese Americans; the evolution of a subculture. 2d ed. Prentice-Hall. '76.

Kraus, Michael. Immigration, the American mosaic; from Pilgrims to modern refugees. Van Nostrand. '66.

LaGumina, S. J. and Cavaioli, F. J. The ethnic dimension in American society. Holbrook Press. '74.

Left Handed. Son of Old Man Hat: a Navaho autobiography recorded by Walter Dyk. University of Nebraska Press. '67.

Levine, L. W. Black culture and black consciousness: Afro-American folk thought from slavery to freedom. Oxford University Press. '78.

Levitan, S. A. and others. Still a dream; the changing status of blacks since 1960. Harvard University Press. '75.

Melendy, H. B. The oriental Americans. Hippocrene Books. '72.

*Metzker, Isaac, ed. A Bintel brief; sixty years of letters from the lower East Side to The Jewish daily Forward. Doubleday. '71.

Moore, J. W. and Pachon, Harry. Mexican Americans. 2d ed. Prentice-Hall. '76.

Myrdal, Gunnar. An American dilemma. Harper. '44; paper ed. Pantheon Books. '75. 2v.

Novak, Michael. The rise of the unmeltable ethnics; politics and culture in the seventies. Macmillan. '73.

O'Connor, Richard. The German-Americans; an informal history. Little, Brown. '68.

Oswalt, W. H. This land was theirs: a study of North American Indians. Wiley. '78.

Patterson, Orlando. Ethnic chauvinism: the reactionary impulse. Stein & Day. '77.

Peachey, Paul and Mudd, Sister Rita, eds. Evolving patterns of ethnicity in American life. National Center for Urban Ethnic Affairs. 1521 16th St. N.W. Washington, DC 20036. '71.

Pennar, Jaan and others, eds. The Estonians in America, 1627-1975; a chronology & fact book. (Ethnic Chronology Series, no17) Oceana Publications. '75.

Pinkney, Alphonso. Black Americans. 2d ed. Prentice-Hall. '75.

Ryan, J. A. ed. White ethnics: their life in working class America. Prentice-Hall. '75.

Saloutos, Theodore. The Greeks in the United States. Harvard University Press. '64.

Schrag, Peter. The decline of the WASP. Simon & Schuster. '73.

Senungetuk, J. E. Give or take a century: an Eskimo chronicle. Indian Historian Press. '71.

Spencer, R. F. and others. The native Americans. Harper. '77.

Stalvey, L. M. The education of a WASP. Morrow. '70.

Steiner, Stanley. The new Indians. Harper & Row. '68.

*Stensland, A. L. Literature by and about the American Indian; an annotated bibliography for junior and senior high school students. National Council of Teachers of English. 1111 Kenyon Rd. Urbana, IL 61801. '73.

Sung, B. L. Mountain of gold; the story of the Chinese in America. Macmillan. '67.
   Paper edition entitled: The story of the Chinese in America. Collier Books. '71.

Széplaki, Joseph, ed. The Hungarians in America, 1583-1974; a chronology & fact book. (Ethnic Chronology Series, no18) Oceana Publications. '75.

Wagley, Charles and Harris, Marvin. Minorities in the New World. Columbia University Press. '58.

Wax, M. L. Indian Americans; unity and diversity. Prentice-Hall. '71.

Weed, P. L. The white ethnic movement and ethnic politics. Praeger. '73.

Wertsman, Vladimir, ed. The Romanians in America, 1748-1974; a chronology and fact book. (Ethnic Chronology Series, no19) Oceana Publications. '75.

Wheeler, T. C. ed. The immigrant experience; the anguish of becoming American. Penguin. '72.

PERIODICALS

*AICH Newsletter. v 7, no 3. Ap. '78.
   Reprinted in this book: New York is a reservation city. M. S. Hines; I'm from a reservation. D. K. Good Elk.

*American Scholar. 45:360-73. Summer '76. Whither integration? Martin Kilson.
   Same: Civil Rights Digest. 8:20–9. Summer '76.

Antioch Review. N. '71. Special issue: The rediscovery of diversity.

Business Week. p 48-53. My. 29. '71. Chicanos campaign for a better deal.

Center Magazine. 7:17-73. Jl. '74. New ethnicity [symposium].

Center Magazine. 7:18-25. Jl. '74. The new ethnicity. Michael Novak.

Center Magazine. 7:26-30. Jl. '74. The case against romantic ethnicity. Gunnar Myrdal.

Center Magazine. 7:31-43. Jl. '74. Italian Americans. Rudolph Vecoli.

Center Magazine. 7:44-50. Jl. '74. After the ethnic experience. J. H. Blake.

Center Magazine. 7:51-66. Jl. '74. National character and community. N. I. Huggins.

Center Magazine. 7:67-73. Jl. '74. Another American dilemma. John Higham.

Christian Century. 93:915-17. O. 27. '76. Ethnics: more-liberal-than-thou. Michael Novak.

Christian Century. 94:718-21. Ag. 17, '77. Troubling future of ethnicity. Philip Perlmutter.

Civil Rights Digest. 3:22-7. Winter '70. Pride and prejudice: a Mexican American dilemma. Edward Casavantes.

Civil Rights Digest. 3:28-31. Winter '70. Will the real Mexican American please stand up? Philip Montez.

Civil Rights Digest. 6:20-7. Spring '74. Puertoriquenas in the United States: the impact of double discrimination. L. M. King.

Civil Rights Digest. 6:29-35. Spring '74. Native women today: sexism and the Indian woman. S. H. Witt.

Civil Rights Digest. 6:36-42. Spring '74. Chicanas and the women's rights movement. Consuelo Nieto.

Civil Rights Digest. 6:46-7. Spring '74. Chinese immigrants. Betty Jung.

*Civil Rights Digest. 6:48-53. Spring '74. Issei: the first women. Emma Gee.

Civil Rights Digest. 8:39-45. Summer '76. The brave-hearted women: the struggle at Wounded Knee. S. H. Witt.

Commentary. 58:55-9. S. '74. Ethnicity and the schools. Nathan Glazer.
Discussion. Commentary. 58:26+. D. '74.

Commentary. 58:33-9. O. '74; 59:10. Ja. '75. Why ethnicity? Nathan Glazer and D. P. Moynihan.
Discussion. Commentary. 59:4+. Ja. '75.

*Commentary. 62:70+. D. '76. Family chronicle. D. H. Donald.
Review of Alex Haley's Roots: the saga of an American family.

Commonweal. 41:534-7. Mr. 16, '45. You can't marry a Filipino. I. B. Buaken.

*Cultures. v 3, no 3:13-27. '76. Cultural trends III, American themes, art and science: The shaping of a people, the United States of America. G. W. Pierson.

Daedalus. Spring '61. Special issue: Ethnic groups in American life.

*Ebony. 32:83-6. Ja. '77. Annual progress report: 1976, the year of the black voter. Alex Poinsett.

Ebony. 32:33-6+. Ap. '77. Alex Haley: the man behind Roots
   H. J. Massaquoi.
Ebony. 32:54-6+. S. '77. Great moments in black history No. XII
   The day the black revolution began. Lerone Bennett Jr.
*Editorial Research Reports. v 1, no 3:47-64. Ja. 20, '71. Ethnic
   America. R. C. Schroeder.
Editorial Research Reports. v 2, no 22:927-44. D. 13, '74. The new
   immigration. Sandra Stencel.
*Editorial Research Reports. v 2, no 7:619-36. Ag. 19, '77. Bi-
   lingual education. Sandra Stencel.
*Education Digest. 40:21-3. Ap. '75. Cultural pluralism and the
   schools [condensed]. J. A. Banks.
      Same in Spanish. Education Digest. 40:24-7. Ap. '75.
      Original version: Educational Leadership. 32:163-6. D. '74.
English Journal. 65:83-7. F. '76. Overview of Chicano folklore.
   R. L. Garcia.
Esquire. 74:107-9+. Ag. '70. The new Indian. Roy Bongartz.
Esquire. 74:110-11+. Ag. '70. Superjew. Roy Bongartz.
Holiday. 58:24-6+. Ap. '77. Great American melting pot. H. M.
   Petrakis and Bobby Vinton.
Indian Historian. 8:54-6. Spring '75. Prison and native people.
   F. D. Black Horse.
Indian Historian. 8:26-31. Summer '75. Among Arizona Indians
   . . . fewer red apples. Ann Patterson.
International Migration Review. v 2, no 2. Spring '68. Special is-
   sue: The Puerto Rican experience on the United States main-
   land.
Journal of Black Studies. 6:401-20. Je. '76. The dozens: an Afri-
   can-heritage theory. Amuzie Chimezie.
Ms. 5:77-80+. Jl. '76. We will remember survival school: a visit
   with women and children of the American Indian movement.
   Susan Braudy.
*New Republic. 176:17-19. Je. 25, '77. Limits of ethnicity. Irving
   Howe.
      Adapted from commencement address at Queens College, New York City.
*New York Times. p C 17. Je. 30, '77. Books of the Times: review
   of Wasp, where is thy sting? by Florence King. R. R. Linge-
   man.
New York Times. p D 7+. Ag. 28, '77. Will "cultural apartheid"
   poison the arts in America? Donal Henahan.
*New York Times. p C 24. O. 7, '77. Astoria, the largest Greek
   city outside Greece. Murray Schumach.
New York Times. p 17. F. 20, '78. Hidden dangers in the ethnic
   revival. Orlando Patterson.
New York Times. p A 16. My. 8, '78. Whale quotas threaten
   Eskimo tradition as well as food supply.
New York Times. p 26. My. 9, '78. Doubts about bilingual educa-
   tion raised in a study released by U.S.

New York Times Magazine. p 37-8+. Je. 7, '64. Explanation of the black psyche. J. O. Killens.

New York Times Magazine. p 82+. D. 8, '68. Soul story. Adrian Dove.

New York Times Magazine. p 32-3+. Mr. 8, '70. This country was a lot better off when the Indians were running it. Vine Deloria Jr.

New Yorker. 48:28-31. My. 27, '72. Speaks with sharp tongue; views of Kahn-Tineta Horn. William Whitworth.

*Newsweek. p 32-3+. D. 21, '70. Ethnic power. Charles Roberts.

Phylon; the Atlanta University Review of Race and Culture. 36:140-8. Je. '75. Ethnicity and cultural pluralism. Israel Rubin.

*Public Interest. 45:20-36. Fall '76. Ethnic miracle. A. M. Greeley.

Scandinavian Review. 64:16-26. Mr. '76. Finns from Alaska to Florida. E. E. Paananen.

Scandinavian Review. 64:55-63. Mr. '76. Danish legacy in America. H. E. Neal.

Scandinavian Review. 64:15-20. Je. '76. Swedish connection. Wesley Westerberg.

Scandinavian Review. 64:39-41. S. '76. Icelanders in the United States. Valdimar Björnson.

Society. 12:14-74. Ja. '75. Ethnic factor: symposium.

*Society. 13:48-74. N. '75. Immigrant parents and native children [symposium].
   Reprinted in this book: Confessions of a third-generation Italian American. W. V. D'Antonio. p 57-63.

Time. 95:13-16+. Ap. 6, '70. Black America, 1970 [symposium].

Time. 106:57. D. 8, '75. Ethnics all.